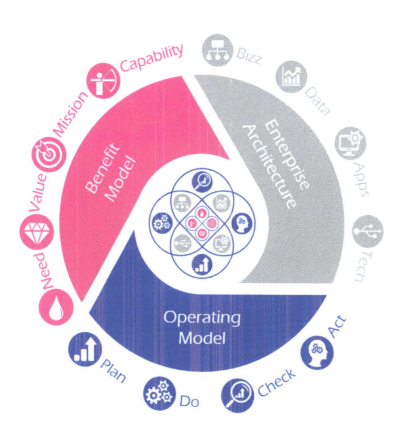

IT for Business (IT4B)

From genesis to revolution – a business and IT approach to digital transformation

IT for Business (IT4B)

From genesis to revolution – a business and IT approach to digital transformation

BRIAN JOHNSON
AND
WALTER ZONDERVAN

IT Governance Publishing

IT Governance Publishing Ltd
Unit 3, Clive Court
Bartholomew's Walk
Cambridgeshire Business Park
Ely
Cambridgeshire
CB7 4EA
United Kingdom
www.itgovernancepublishing.co.uk

First published in the United Kingdom in 2018 by IT Governance Publishing.

ISBN: 978-1-84928-999-3

FOREWORD

One of this book's reviewers wrote that in business there are very few, if any, readymade answers. That comment deserves to be placed upfront because this book is based entirely on that point and raises questions and provides insights based on experience.

There are no readymade answers because businesses have different goals and different cultures, and there is no 'go-to' list of solutions that can be applied without effort or thought. This book serves to identify many of the common issues that businesses face and provide advice about how they might be solved; it does not promote one framework or method, but illustrates that most frameworks are not designed to be all-encompassing and that many different good practices need to be used to help IT manage changes that impact the way that enterprises carry out business processes.

Myriad 'IT frameworks' and 'methods' exist that are often applied as a one-stop shop to address any business or IT issue because there is no clear understanding about where the framework is of most use, or where it is of least value. IT4B does not reinvent any of the methods, alter their definitions or claim to do anything radically different except to provide a coherent understanding of your enterprise's digital readiness.

So, why buy into it if nothing is new? Well, do you really want another variant of ITIL® or COBIT®? Will different definitions of governance or risk really improve the development of new IT-driven services? Or would you like to read about how to order well-known concepts, methods and processes in a way that focuses digital innovation on the business? Business processes drive business change, and automating these business processes is the means to providing IT services that (hopefully) make things more efficient; IT processes simply provide support. This book is intended to focus on the needs of the business first and foremost.

Readiness is a key issue. Readiness is based on capability and the desire to improve business (most often involving eye-watering investment in technology), although a cultural determination is most often the crucial factor in success. As another reviewer pointed out, this approach leads to a clear understanding about how operational goals drive the business direction and impact governance and strategy.

In terms of content, anything you see in a box is stuff you might find interesting but does not directly affect the IT4B approach. And appendices are provided to amplify some issues for those wishing to get to grips with details. Nothing in this book changes or reinvents existing best practices; the IT4B approach identifies common elements and places them in a context that helps you think about dependencies. And the book is a conversation, not a dogma.

To begin with, we want to look at improvement in artistic capabilities over the centuries, which evidence suggests was based on technology, not talent. If that does not convince you that the book is not an 'IT method', not much else will!

ABOUT THE AUTHORS

Brian Johnson has held a number of key leadership and strategic roles in government and private companies. He was a part of the UK government team that created the ITIL approach. He has written a number of books on ITIL, the software life cycle and the role of IT in business. When he isn't working or writing, Brian's passion is playing football.

Walter Zondervan is a digital innovator who is always looking to help organisations reach their full potential. In his 20+ years of experience, he became fascinated with translating business goals into IT strategy. As a digital transformation strategist, he developed a comprehensive approach to this, which has been partially adopted by the BiSL® Next framework for business information management.

Working together on BiSL® Next, the authors decided to take it a step further and combine their insights to create a practical IT4B approach to digital transformation.

ACKNOWLEDGEMENTS

IT Governance Publishing for being the most helpful publisher on the planet, the anonymous and very helpful IT Governance Publishing reviewers, and Maarten Hillenaar for coming up with the IT4B acronym.

CONTENTS

Contents

Contents

Contents

TECHNOLOGY TRANSFORMING ART

Hockney on IT4B

This book is focused on the role of innovation in business and society rather than just the invention of yet another model. The model-centric among you can skip this light entertainment and hold your breath for the chapters when we expand the IT4B elements. That said, if you miss this introduction, you will miss out on discovering how technology has transformed society in the past and how an artist and cultural icon discovered that art might also be a science.

Now, what did David Hockney, said artist and cultural icon, do for us to include his name in a piece about some approach to innovation thrown up by a pair of business analysts who want to make business goals the key to innovation in IT?

Hockney and the 15th-century painting transformation

Hockney wondered if the enormous jumps in clarity and composition (not to say perspective) achieved by European painters after the Middle Ages were brought about by technology, in particular by the use of mirrors and lenses.

In the late Middle Ages (Hockney dated the transformation as 1420) something radical happened to the art of painting. Almost overnight, the appearance of paintings changed from cartoonish to near photographic accuracy.

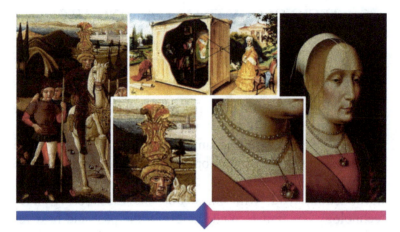

Figure 1: The 15th-century painting transformation

Science was not exactly popular in the Middle Ages. It was largely considered magic or witchery, and holding any belief where science was the proponent (astronomy, for example) or questioning accepted norms (such as slavery, women's rights and creationism) led to the inquisition.

Hockney's *Secret Knowledge* presents a theory (backed up by illustrations from artists in the Middle Ages) that suggests everyone who painted before, say, 1450 was in control of the local torture chamber, thereby ensuring that no one laughed aloud and pointed out that the artist had the talent of a pre-cataract surgery chimp. Hockney's Secret Knowledge presents a theory (backed up by illustrations from artists in the Middle Ages) that suggests everyone who painted before, say, 1450 was in control of the local torture chamber, thereby ensuring that no one laughed aloud and pointed out that the artist had the talent of a pre-cataract surgery chimp (or that the general public would accept any tripe so long as it was created by somebody featured in whatever passed for Twitter. Probably everyone gave the town crier a piece of parchment with one very large gilt character on it and 139 small ones…).

After 1450, the quality of paintings vastly improved, and it is likely that optical devices to project images were to thank. David Hockney[1] and physicist Charles M. Falco[2] claim that the advances in realism[3] and accuracy were primarily the result of optical instruments[4], such as the *camera obscura*[5], *camera lucida*[6] and curved mirrors[7], rather than solely due to the development of artistic[8] technique and skill. Hockney analysed the work of the Old Masters[9] and argued that their level of accuracy is impossible to create by *plein air* painting.

Caravaggio was most likely the first to use a *camera obscura* (Hockney cites a lot of evidence in support) and Vermeer clearly used optics extensively. The art world was turned upside down (though it remained flat to avoid stake-burning episodes). In fact at one point, the images projected would have been upside down; at one time even reversed (another proof-point for Hockney in that an astonishing number of artistic models appear to be left handed in many works. True, being left handed might have been more common in 1300, but given that left handed people could very easily be taken to be witches or warlocks, it seems a bit unlikely).

---

[1] https://en.wikipedia.org/wiki/David_Hockney
[2] https://en.wikipedia.org/wiki/Charles_M._Falco
[3] https://en.wikipedia.org/wiki/Realism_(arts)
[4] https://en.wikipedia.org/wiki/Optical_instrument
[5] https://en.wikipedia.org/wiki/Camera_obscura
[6] https://en.wikipedia.org/wiki/Camera_lucida
[7] https://en.wikipedia.org/wiki/Curved_mirror
[8] https://en.wikipedia.org/wiki/Artist
[9] https://en.wikipedia.org/wiki/Old_Master

New ideas, methods and technologies were focused in a way that had not been considered before. After 1600 or so, the photographic level of detail is astonishing in many works (see Figure 2).

Figure 2: Photograph or painting?

We think this illustrates that technology leaps do promote innovation. If the Hockney–Falco thesis is true, what lessons can be learned from this medieval "digital transformation" that disrupted the art of painting six centuries ago? First, it is an example of how new technology found its application in an existing field. What followed was a revolutionary change in the production process of paintings, a revolutionary increase in production speed and a revolutionary decrease in production cost, which made paintings available to a broader audience than the usual priests and kings. Andy Warhol, eat your heart out.

For us, IT4B is not of itself an innovation. Like a drawing on paper or a painting on canvas, it is an instantiation of something at a given point – IT4B provides a snapshot of 'where are you now' in relation to your enterprise's digital aspirations. The IT4B concepts and methods can be used as a 'successful delivery toolkit'; think of it as a 21st-century *camera obscura* that can be used to focus new ideas and technologies to help the business achieve goals more rapidly and efficiently.

How is IT4B used?

The icon on the left of Figure 3 represents operational services, the central icon represents the 'IT4B lens through which current business is assessed for 'readiness'' and the colourful projection on the right illustrates the outputs from using the 'lens'. These outputs are assessments of the enterprise capability in 16 key elements that you will find discussed in just about every IT method known. So, Figure 3 shows the basic parameters for the IT4B model. Throughout the book, we will expand on the elements and on the capabilities needed in the enterprise to achieve digital goals.

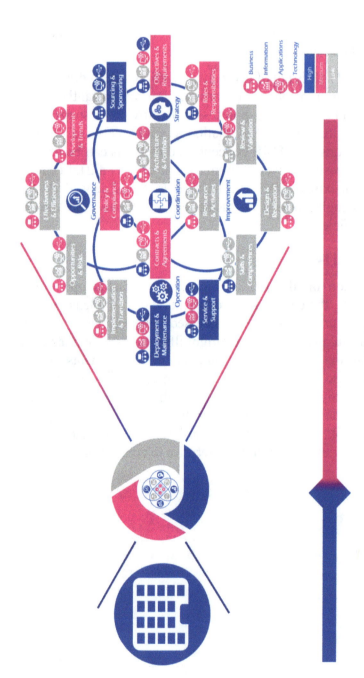

Figure 3: The IT4B *camera obscura*

IT4B provides an assessment of readiness based on identifying necessary capabilities and the degree to which they exist in the enterprise. Capabilities may need to exist at different levels of expertise depending on the nature of business transformations, and a simple 'high, medium, low' stratification is used to assist in visualising results.

Sceptics can check out more information on the Hockney–Falco thesis on Wikipedia[10].

Lessons learned from the 15th-century painting transformation:

- New technology applied in existing field.
- Revolutionary change in process.
- Revolutionary increase in speed.
- Revolutionary decrease in cost.
- Availability to a broader audience.

Do any of these ring a bell in the 21st century?

---

[10] https://en.wikipedia.org/wiki/Hockney%E2%80%93Falco_thesis

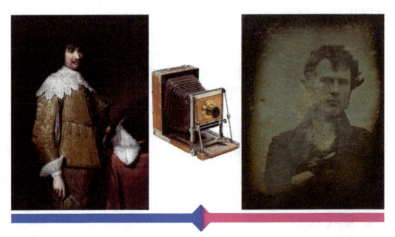

Figure 4: The next revolution – Robert Cornelius' Self-Portrait: The First Ever "Selfie" (1839)

CHAPTER ONE: FROM GENESIS TO REVOLUTION

Que sera, sera, what will IT4B...

What is IT4B? It sounds like another acronym designed by IT to fool the business into thinking IT is of vague interest to the business community. Well, this is IT for business, to help the business side of the house determine whether IT is 'aligned' or 'integrated', and what is missing (and something will always be missing). Of course, when it comes to the digitisation of information services, IT will be in the driver's seat, meaning IT4B becomes a tool for both parties to determine gaps in requirements, competence, capabilities and even knowledge of the various methods needed to move from business-designed objectives to IT-delivered services.

The primary goal is to assess the readiness of the business and its IT support to achieve business goals. Business goals are supported by business processes; in regulated markets that depend on IT for efficiency, there is not a lot of point in implementing an IT method before identifying what needs to be achieved by the business.

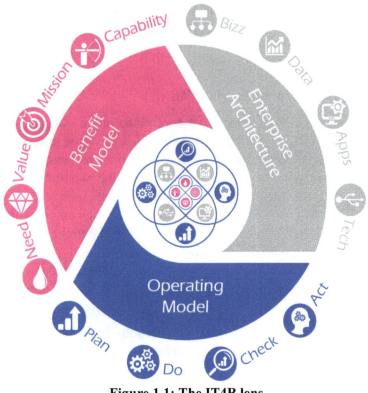

Figure 1.1: The IT4B lens

Figure 1.1 illustrates the subject areas covered by this way of thinking. IT4B is a structured way of thinking, supported by detailed examination of the most common attributes in an enterprise. As described in the introduction, this is the lens, a model through which we examine business and IT readiness. Three linked components – the Benefit Model, the Enterprise Architecture and the Operating Model – are used to focus the issues illustrated around the circumference of the model. In the centre, the icons we use to describe elements that always need attention are shown; these elements will be identified later. For now, this chapter introduces the model and the reason we built it, and outlines what will be discussed later.

Providing the necessary structure to facilitate digital innovation is often a challenge. Based on our more than 20 years of research and experience at the interface of business and IT, an approach emerged that helps translate business goals into digital 'ambitions' and a roadmap in a practical (non-technical) manner. Using a set of simple canvasses, you gain insight into the steps you can take to transform your organisation into a digital enterprise.

As we mentioned it is not a 'new' IT method; existing good practice methods are referenced, not altered, and we explain how they can work more effectively when used together.

The focus is the realisation of the opportunity that IT presents. If only your IT 'innovation' was focused on the future of the business and the business market in which it operates rather than implementing the latest method, software or technology.

More often than not, your IT people expect you to understand their language and claim that it is impossible for the business to articulate what they need or want. Most, if not all, of the IT frameworks and models don't help with 'translation' of business requirements. The result is that a rapid response to a business problem is most often based on finding help in one of the IT best practices familiar to the enterprise.

In these circumstances, IT is a roadblock to innovation. Instead of examining the principles of, say, efficiency and effectiveness in relation to how quickly they can respond to the business when new services are needed or in times of crisis, the default response is to examine their various models of best practices to see where they fit into a process they understand.

The philosophy behind IT4B is that the full potential of digital innovation (Figure 1.2) can only be achieved if it is successfully embedded within a benefit model, an enterprise architecture and your enterprise's operating model. On the other hand, the true power of digital innovation can only be fully enjoyed if your enterprise has reached a certain level of digital readiness. The foundation of successful digital transformation is constructed when there is equilibrium between digital readiness and digital innovation. The IT4B framework and canvasses enable enterprises to discover the opportunities for digital innovation and create a digital profile of their specific enterprise. The goal is to illustrate how to use the model and the myriad methods that exist in IT to reach the appropriate level of digital readiness.

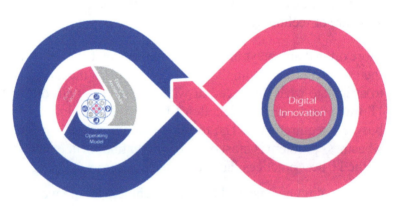

Figure 1.2: Digital innovation

No one in IT ever tries to do a bad job or provide poor customer service; the issue is that IT professionals are most often directly recruited and are therefore intrinsically IT-centric – they have no experience of the business in which they operate and thus seem distanced from understanding what is going on. Consider again the issue of regulated markets: who would you expect to be the subject-matter expert? It certainly would not be the people running the data centre.

Discovering the missing pieces is often a navel-gazing IT exercise, which arrives at a number of fairly standard responses. We need our IT people to be certified in architecture, or a development method, or a programming method, or a method to manage projects. Often the result requires significant management attention and the entire enterprise is said to be in need of some form of recognised external audit badge, or sometimes more money to buy more 'tools'.

It is not focused on making sure IT understands business.

Figure 1.3: Using both halves of the brain for business and IT

Just as the focus for healthcare should be the health of the population, the focus of every digital innovation should be 'business first'.

Business-first approaches require insight into the enterprise and its processes. It can be helpful to take a bimodal approach to the business processes by discerning two distinctive categories: 'left-brain' processes (logic, analytic, linear, mathematical, facts) and 'right-brain' processes (creative, imagination, holistic, visual, experience). This is shown in Figure 1.3, which illustrates having to keep opposing and often contradictory arguments at the same time in different parts of the brain.

In the early days of IT, the focus was almost entirely on supporting 'left-brain' processes. Nowadays, 'right-brain' solutions are being hyped. However, both types of processes deserve equal attention to achieve a well-balanced functional fit.

Business first also should mean that discussions about IT should take place after the business requirement is fully understood.

Figure 1.4: Balancing the high-level concerns

The first step in understanding the lens and the IT4B approach is context. When it comes to digital innovation, balance is everything, which is why it's one of the key principles of the IT4B framework. Let's begin with an explanation of the icons at the centre of the lens model. At the heart of the lens, we find a representation of the enterprise benefit model (Figure 1.4) as a balance between 'need' and 'value', and 'mission' and 'capability'. This can be a customer need and a business value proposition as well as a public need and a public value proposition.

Mission and Capability are often in tension: without the necessary capabilities, any mission is impossible. Similarly, Need and Value are in tension: what is needed is often not valued and vice versa. For example, the business might need block chain technology, as many logistics businesses have discovered, but the value is the elimination of the business problems that have plagued shipping for many years, not the technology.

The benefit model is applicable to both profit and non-profit enterprises. There also needs to be a balance between an enterprise mission and the required capabilities to achieve these goals. The benefit model helps you to gain insight into the challenges an enterprise faces and is the first step in designing a strategy for digital innovation.

Figure 1.5: Multiple perspectives

Next, we consider the perspectives that will be addressed when innovating business services. The step is to perceive the lens model in context: business, information, applications (services) and technology (Figure 1.5). The degree of impact of each of these perspectives will alter depending on where you are in terms of thinking about new business. When discussing new ideas, business requirements have absolute priority, though, of course, the potential of technology will be discussed. At the other end of the scale, when operations are running 'business as usual' then technology might be the most important perspective.

With a fully **visualised** enterprise architecture, the likely impact of any business decision or (digital) innovation can be illustrated quickly; the iconography is intended to be aesthetically pleasing and simple to follow.

Nowadays, all enterprises use IT in many forms. Some even use IT for purposes other than updating Facebook or tweeting. A digital enterprise goes way beyond just using IT as a business enabler; it has basically merged the primary business process(es) with IT. Who ever thought that a taxi ride (Uber) would become a digital service? Or an overnight stay (Airbnb)? However, there is rarely a digital transformation that starts from a greenfield situation.

Taking Tiger Mountain (by Strategy)

This section discusses business and IT digital services.

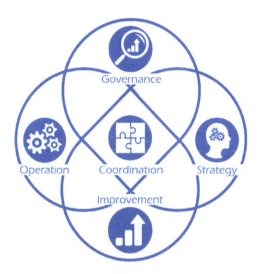

Figure 1.6: IT4B quadrants

No matter how 'digital' a transformation might be, there is still the important human factor to consider. Successful digital transformation requires a certain level of digital readiness of the enterprise itself. How do we work together with regard to the business, information, applications and technology perspectives? The good old PDCA cycle can come in handy.

The IT4B operating model requires you to adopt four orphans*, which are illustrated as overlapping circles (Figure 1.6): governance, strategy, improvement and operation (labels and hieroglyphs shown). Within each quadrant you can use the PDCA cycle to identify what should be improved. In this way, the operating model canvas will be used to create a digital profile showing the readiness of your enterprise for digital transformation.

The IT4B framework can provide guidelines for digital transformation by representing a well-balanced benefit model, fitted in a supporting enterprise architecture and run by a digitisation-ready operating model. In Figure 1.7 you can see that all three of the previous 'models' are now joined up in this 'continuous improvement' model and all the models are interrelated.

Think of four quadrants that represent key business and IT components, four perspectives on these quadrants and four balancing elements that all must come together to ensure the business mission can be supported. Once you have grasped this explanation you are off and running!

*Why orphans? Well, governance, strategy, improvement and operation are most often the subject of individual guidance. And yet everywhere you'll find that they are linked and actions taken in one area very much affect another.

Figure 1.7: Everything joins up somewhere

In the next chapter, we will discuss more of the concepts in relation to equilibrium and balance.

Coordination

Policy & Compliance

Contracts & Agreements

Architecture & Portfolio

Resources & Activities

 ... from a business service perspective
 ... from an information service perspective
 ... from an application service perspective
 ... from a technology service perspective

CHAPTER TWO: IT'S A QUESTION OF BALANCE

The heart of the matter: what makes your enterprise 'tick'?

Expanding the concepts

Unsurprisingly, we have selected domain names that relate to recognised practices. In many models the word 'Change' is used, but we have opted for 'Improvement' for two reasons: change is often resisted as being unwanted, and who does not want to improve? Even Ronaldo and Messi train.

For anyone interested in knowing how we started to think about the need for a lens through which to assess digital readiness, take a look at Appendix A.

Starting with Figure 2.1, introduced in Chapter one, think about the environment in which a business operates.

Continuous improvement is sought, in increased revenues (and profits) or just in the enterprise's efficiencies and effectiveness where money is not the making of the business.

The enterprise needs to deploy services in line with the business mission and capabilities to harvest benefits, fulfil business needs and create or maintain business value. And as mentioned, multiple perspectives need to be applied to all components of the enterprise architecture in order to maintain an equilibrium and, of course, to satisfy the stakeholders in the enterprise that business operations are running smoothly and can be incrementally improved as needed.

In the centre of that expanding universe, we placed icons that together form the IT4B model. This is expanded to identify 16 key elements (four for each quadrant in the central model) that are the focus for a million different best practices – rarely discussed as part of a holistic approach to using IT to drive business changes successfully.

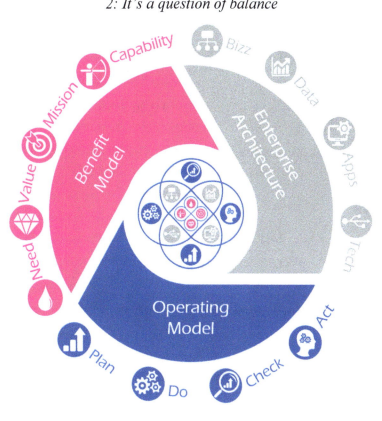

Figure 2.1: The IT4B universe

Why did we build it? Well, because no one else seemed to have looked at the range of existing best practices in the IT universe and bothered to put them together in a framework for the business (and IT) to use to drive digital transformation.

As with all good universes, this IT4B universe expands.

The camera obscura for business and IT

Having outlined why the model was built (Chapter one) and how it was put together, we now need to get into more detail about its practical use. The use of the 'camera obscura' for examining business issues in relation to IT came about when the penny finally dropped that every time business people were consulted about IT and digitisation, they drifted off to sleep.

Now, let's join up what we discussed in Chapter one.

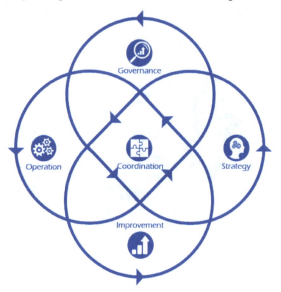

Figure 2.2: The gyroscope.

(Place a finger or a pencil or anything pointy anywhere on the gyroscope, move it in any direction and you will see how it works)

The IT4B operating model is navigated using the 'gyroscope' – our term for the model of continuous improvement as a guideline along all of the 16 elements (Figure 3.5). The gyroscope is clearly formed by one continuous line that develops four intersecting (interlocking in most respects) circles described as Governance, Strategy,

Improvement and Operation. If you are familiar with the Business Information Services Library (BiSL) or collaborative business service design, the concept of identifying and describing four related 'spheres' to establish a plan-do-check (study)-act way of looking at related issues should ring a few bells.

Before opening up the IT4B model, we wish to make clear the difference between outcomes and outputs. Outcome is what the business needs and values and is directly related to benefit, whereas output is often a delivery mechanism or digital service or even a product that enables operational activities to perform the necessary work to what contributes to successful outcomes. Keep in mind that an application or service is not an output; mistakes are often made when thinking about digital transformation when the shiny new application that counts beans is assumed to be the same thing as the business need to manage inventory 'just-in-time'.

In subsequent chapters, we will follow a logical structure of discussing the domain quadrant (as labelled in the 'gyroscope'), the touchstone elements (particularly the touchstone element considered most important to business outcomes in that domain) and the three other elements that contribute to the output of each domain. The touchstone elements are the capabilities viewed through our camera obscura.

In Figure 2.3 we summarise these elements that we think are the mission-critical activities in any enterprise; shown in blue are four central 'touchstone elements', or activities that focus directly on the enterprise existence, and shown in grey are the widely recognised 'common elements' or activities that you will find essential to supporting the core activities. The underlying skeleton of the model is shown to emphasise that the touchstone elements are principally found in specific domains of a model that resembles a gyroscope.

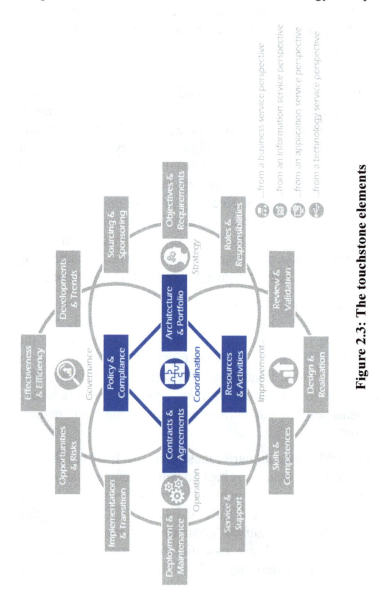

Figure 2.3: The touchstone elements

The major strength of using the model is in aligning goal setting with operation. This balance is necessary to ensure the business needs are fully understood and supported by using IT.

IT4B is intended to be used in balancing resources, maintaining equilibrium and identifying what is needed to transform business using that horrible IT stuff.

For each of the four overlapping circles (Governance, Strategy, Improvement and Operation) there are four elements that comprise the concepts that we think must be in equilibrium. Each of the elements (and the touchstone elements) should be considered in the context of four perspectives: business, information (or data), applications (or services) and, of course, technology in order to obtain a rounded picture of digital transformation effort.

In the Governance circle or quadrant, the overall goal, *Effectiveness & Efficiency*, must be in balance with overall *Policy & Compliance*. And the *Opportunities & Risks* facing the enterprise must be in balance *with Developments & Trends* in the environment in which the enterprise operates. In the Governance quadrant, the business perspective and the strategy perspective will inevitably be more important than improvement and operation, but these two perspectives will increase in importance the further the enterprise proceeds with ideas for digitisation.

Further, these elements form the underpinning structure for the support of the business needs and values that are fundamental to fulfilling the business mission and the capabilities needed to do so.

Being IT types (albeit having at least worked in the real world of business for long enough to know that business cares not a jot about the latest IT 'models' or 'methods'), of course we had to build our own model. The only difference between 'ours' and another model is we have not tried to reinvent methods or create buzzwords; the model just tries to offer a coherent picture of the key issues and competences that any enterprise will need if it is dependent on IT.

The approach (or way of thinking) is to discover which elements or resources are in good shape and which are not, and then make reasoned arguments about what needs to be done, what should be done and what are the necessary actions to take.

IT4B assists in the assessment of what you need to focus upon in order to help your enterprise prosper, provide better services, or, at the basic level, simply decide how IT can really help create a better digital future.

Further, these elements form the underpinning structure for the support of the business needs and values that are fundamental to fulfilling business *Mission* and the *Capabilities* needed to do so.

IT4B assists in the assessment of what you need to focus upon in order to help your enterprise prosper, or provide better services or at the basic level simply decide how IT can really help create a better digital future. Keep in mind though that not everyone has an iPhone; not everyone has a home computer and the digital future should not be just for those that can afford it. We expand on these points in later chapters.

Just to whet your appetite, Figure 2.4 provides an example of how the entire 'digital transformation' process comes together, illustrating what you need for digital readiness. As ever, you must find out 'Where are we now?', 'How are we going to get where we need to be?' and 'How will we get there?'.

Figure 2.4: What you need to be ready for digitisation

Governance

Effectiveness & Efficiency

Opportunities & Risks

Developments & Trends

Policy & Compliance

 ... from a business service perspective
 ... from an information service perspective
 ... from an application service perspective
 ... from a technology service perspective

CHAPTER THREE: THE 'ROMAN RIDING' OF GOVERNANCE

How to be highly effective while being compliant?

How to adopt new developments while mitigating their risk?

Governance is not the same as management

When it comes to discussing digital transformation, the central question for board members is often 'How to be highly effective and compliant at the same time versus how to take full advantage of new developments while mitigating their risks?'. The answer is to think about the enterprise holistically, employing well-known activities in a framework rather than as piecemeal, silo-driven exercises.

The role of Governance here should be an enabling role, balancing opportunity and risk to benefit the enterprise. Governance should also include the issues of scaling and speed of delivery. Business advantage often depends on speed to market.

Governance is not the same as management (though in order to govern effectively it is often necessary to be a good manager). First, let's refresh your memory with one of the accepted definitions of Governance. Governance (business and IT) is the organisational capacity exercised by the board, executive management and (IT) management to control the formulation and implementation of strategy; where IT is involved (and it usually is), governance is a means of ensuring the fusion of business and IT. The business requires good governance over IT to ensure that desirable behaviour is achieved (Gartner, for example, posits that assignment of decision rights and an accountability framework to encourage desirable behaviour in the use of IT and digital services in general is an essential component).

Governance and Policy, therefore, are integral to management oversight of any overarching enterprise-wide initiatives. Executive decisions will lead to strategic investment, whereas failure to interest executives and to elicit support for improvements will lead to changes being constrained, of limited use and valued only at the operational level.

Outcome (and output)

The Governance sector is primarily (and almost exclusively) focused on business outcome; outputs might be hurled into the discussion by the CIO or those thinking the iPhone is the outcome, but the Mission and Capability of the enterprise to deliver business outcomes is the discussion point when considering business Need and Value. Of course, if discussions also conclude that something is not valued, it is certainly unlikely to be needed.

The most important element with regard to outcome is therefore the enterprise policy and clear understanding of how policy will be enforced to ensure compliance.

In the gyroscope, the central tenet of good governance, *Policy & Compliance*, is focused on enterprise growth through a twin focus on *Opportunities & Risks* and *Developments & Trends*. In turn, these activities contribute to the overall *Effectiveness & Efficiency* of the enterprise by fulfilling the business mission.

Figure 3.1 illustrates that the essential outcome of Governance is *Effectiveness & Efficiency* in the process of validating Outcomes (and to an extent Outputs, i.e. improvements and Requests for Change (RFCs), that in themselves should arise from *Need and Value*, and most likely follow on from some form of analysis of *Developments & Trends*). Necessary developments will inevitably impact the business mission and will almost certainly require a reassessment of the enterprise capabilities. Most likely this will involve a general evaluation of the Operation domain. The pivotal role of *Policy & Compliance* in the centre of the Governance domain cannot be underestimated. As mentioned, it will be necessary to establish a means of ensuring (and proving) compliance; compliance may well be mandatory (some external government or financial body will for sure have mandatory activities) and internal, and in some cases external auditors will need to be employed.

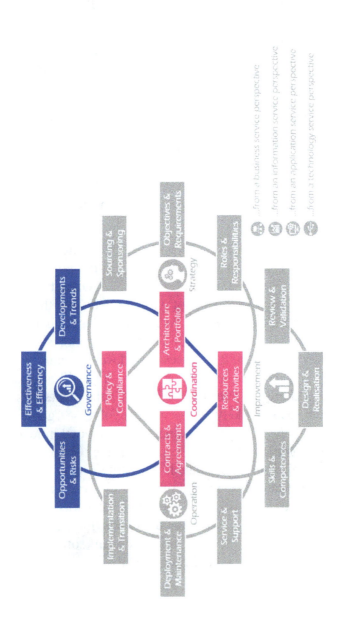

Figure 3.1: Touchstone elements and Governance

3: The 'roman riding' of governance

The influence of the touchstone activities is at the heart of all strategic discussions because of the enormous impact on Operation. Improvement might well start with Operation (because of business needs or recognition of perhaps poorly designed digital services), though the shaping mechanism remains Governance.

Policy & Compliance

Governance

- Specify and document regulations (rules or sets of rules) that govern the supply of products and services
- Ensure that the supply of products and services is compliant with policy

 ... from a business service perspective

 ... from an information service perspective

 ... from an application service perspective

 ... from a technology service perspective

Policy & Compliance

Policies are specified and documented regulations (rules or sets of rules) that govern the supply of systems and services from first principles of identification, planning, development, implementation, operation, improvement and decommissioning. Policies may relate to information services and to information technology and to wider enterprise and management issues. Standards and good practices are not policies. Policies define and govern which standards and good practice can be used; standards and good practice are used to implement policies.

Policies will by necessity impact enterprise *Architecture & Portfolio* in the Strategy domain and how objectives and requirements are taken forward in development of Improvement activities. The services resulting from developing new or improved digital services might well be subject to contractual agreements; contracts with external parties will be established at board level and the issue of compliance will be central.

General issues – for example, standards – are the fundamental points of management policies and these are usually implemented through using good practice, though the specifics of most standards and the implementation and operation thereof is through technical policies. The issues for which governance policies may be required can be categorised as either management or technical.

Policies, of course, can also be considered as either enabling or constraining.

Enabling policies are those that aim to support, promote and encourage the deployment of effective services and information systems. Take a wild guess at what a constraining policy does.

We are not going to reinvent governance. Governance means formal management oversight: how the enterprise is currently managed in terms of hierarchies, authority, roles and responsibilities and so on, and is not really a cultural phenomenon or issue. Governance should focus on:

• The future direction and how well the enterprise is positioned for improving;

• What the priorities are, what makes them priorities and who sets them;

• How the business and business information activities are broken down, and how they are currently undertaken and organised;

• Where and why there is potential for increased efficiency, effectiveness and economy, and how IT management might contribute;

• What the geographic distribution of the enterprise units and business processes is; and

• Information/data architectures that are service-oriented, and implement common architectural and design patterns that lend themselves to greater levels of consistency, reuse and adaptability.

Governance will require setting policy about who does what and who is authorised to do what. A custodian is a person, body or group of individuals (or more probably a number of groups) that is in day- to-day control of digital information services. The digital information services owner, therefore, can delegate responsibilities to a custodian, which may or may not be external, depending on who supplies the services.

Although this delegation may be both necessary and practical, the owner cannot abrogate ultimate responsibility (or accountability) for the security, integrity and confidentiality of the information and the proper functioning of the digital information service. Furthermore, compliance with policy will need to be established, whether by means of internal or external auditing or assessments.

And do not underestimate the cost of compliance (perhaps that should also read the cost of non-compliance).

Activities (a better description at this level of the enterprise than process or procedure) indicates that the policy outcomes should be considered first, and then initiatives should be prioritised against other commitments. Once this has been completed, the stakeholders can be identified and the risks considered for each option. This will enable a preferred option to be selected.

Identifying options, determining the stakeholders and assessing risks is in effect a recursive process that is carried out until one of the options is refined enough to enable the policy objective to be met. More guidance can be found in the IT Governance Publishing book *Collaborative Business Design*[11].

The feedback from this cycle to policy outcomes indicates that it is often necessary to revisit one of the activity steps when the outcome of one of the later steps questions one of the original assumptions or conclusions.

Ultimately, every component should be aligned with the enterprise's strategic goals. Without such alignment, management should question why scarce resources are being

---

[11] www.itgovernancepublishing.co.uk/product/collaborative-business-design

allocated and why the component is being funded. Good governance is essential to allow appropriate strategies to be constructed that will facilitate harvesting the expected benefits of digital transformation. Strategy is so fundamental to constructing the portfolio that any change in strategy will trigger an ad hoc review to ensure that all components remain aligned. When a major change occurs, such as results from an acquisition or market re-enterprise, the enterprise may also review its selection criteria and priorities, along with the full set of components.

Governance therefore has an impact on delivery planning, which comprises assessment of a number of primary activities, examining policy outcomes, risks and list of stakeholders, and identification of a preferred option. The preferred option allows Strategy to further develop concepts to produce a delivery plan.

Developments & Trends

Governance

- Perform market analysis, benchmarking, and research of new developments
- Determine the relevance of new developments for the enterprise
- Identify strategic themes

 ... from a business service perspective

 ... from an information service perspective

 ... from an application service perspective

 ... from a technology service perspective

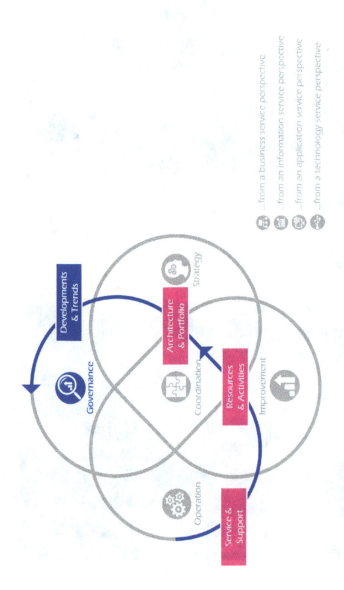

...from a business service perspective

...from an information service perspective

...from an application service perspective

...from a technology service perspective

Figure 3.2: Following developments and trends

Developments & Trends

The enterprise that is not thinking of the future is unlikely to grow. Who said that? Well, we did but no doubt someone more important or much smarter did the same and gets paid more.

Blockchain, big data and gadgets: who gets to decide what the added value for the business could be? Could the application of a new development help the enterprise be even more effective and efficient? Perhaps a development might result in a new value proposition or a new benefit model

Figure 3.2 illustrates the context for *Development and Trends* to explore the market for novel ideas and gadgets and new technologies that might be useful to the enterprise. It is up to those responsible for *Opportunities & Risks* to analyse what the potential benefit would be in terms of new value propositions or impact (positive or negative) on the current benefit model, or maybe even an opportunity for a brand-new benefit model.

Market analysis, benchmarking and research play a significant role in the portfolio management process. An enterprise's portfolio components are driven by such considerations as market opportunity, platform development, support functions, regulatory obligations or operational requirements. Input from the marketing function is required for some of the strategic decisions that dictate criteria to be used in selecting and managing components. For a non-profit enterprise, a similar analysis of value for money or value to organisational vision will be needed for component selection and management. This stage is characterised by a transition from divergent to convergent thinking: from considering the issues that face the enterprise to defining the themes for the activity that will deal with those issues.

Consumers of business services, whether IT driven or steam driven, are often the source of ideas for improvement because they see opportunities, which may be *Developments & Trends*; *Developments & Trends* has the less than surprising role of spotting relevant new developments in business, information, applications and technology. Consumers are not the sole source of trend spotting, of course, as this function is required 'across the board' – including the board.

Many enterprises will survive, perhaps even prosper, without investment, though it should seem clear that like houses, a bit of redecorating now and again rarely goes amiss. In the model, we propose those responsible for *Resources & Activities*, *Architecture & Portfolio* and *Service & Support* should provide the most feedback. This proposal does not absolve the remainder of the enterprise, nor does it imply any organisational changes; how the enterprise is structured is not an element of the proposals, as such changes would be considered an orthogonal issue.

The (reasonably) well-known bimodal architecture model, mentioned in Chapter one, is often used to characterise how the enterprise operates.

The enterprise needs to identify the strategic themes that arise from examination of *Developments & Trend*s.

Identifying strategic themes

Board-level activities in the Governance phase are focused on identifying strategic themes and determining what will shape the enterprise's future direction.

Themes can be regarded as the 'strategy success factors' – the things that the enterprise must get right to achieve its objectives.

They are the areas of activity that will make the most important contributions to supporting or promoting the business, management or organisational changes and improvements sought by the enterprise in the near future.

A theme is a grouping of developments and other changes that will help to take the enterprise forward in pursuit of its business strategy and objectives.

A theme may focus on particular strategic strands, such as e-business, but if it does it will also recognise other strands, such as changes in enterprise, business processes, responsibilities, working methods and procedures, management and technical policies, administrative support, external relationships and so on. Even a theme that is primarily focused on IT will touch on other strands in the enterprise; IT can never be considered in isolation from the business.

A theme in the strategy will be a significant topic, related to strategic change that is of concern to the business management. It is a topic that business management will wish to keep under review for the foreseeable future, as part of the task of monitoring the performance of the business and the achievement of its business objectives. The reviewing of a theme will be the task of those responsible for managing *Opportunities & Risks*. And, of course, those responsible for *Policy & Compliance* will take responsibility for validation.

For the strategy, themes may be expressed in terms of significant changes or developments required in various areas:

- High-level results, such as for government:
    - Policy outcomes;
    - External communications and interworking;
    - Information sharing; and
    - 'Virtual' services.
- New ways of working:
    - Managing the information resource of the enterprise (see also BiSL).
    - Sourcing and procurement issues.
    - Major operational information systems.
    - IT support for redesigned business processes.
    - Improved services.

It should be possible to express the essence of the strategy in no more than half a dozen thoughtful themes. The description of each theme will include:

- The reason why the theme is strategically important;
- The strategic issues that the theme begins to address; and
- The main changes or developments that the enterprise will expect to achieve

Good governance will be key to managing the progress of developments and themes.

Prioritisation and governance

As part of examining the governance dilemma, next we focus on how good governance assists in sorting out the enterprise's priorities. Winnowing the direction from careful assessment of both opportunities and risks is central to establishing the digital future.

Effectiveness & Efficiency

Governance

- Ensure the achievement of the enterprises objectives and requirements
- Ensure that this is achieved using the minimum amount of resources and activities

 ... from a business service perspective

 ... from an information service perspective

 ... from an application service perspective

 ... from a technology service perspective

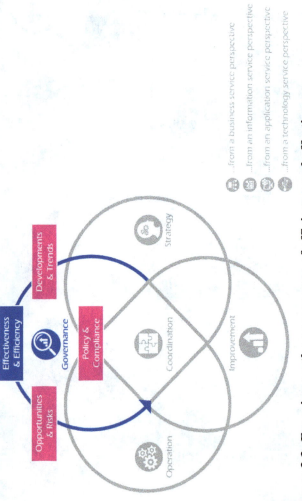

Figure 3.3: Focusing on the governance of efficiency and effectiveness

Effectiveness & Efficiency

The outcome of Governance is now under scrutiny. To put it another way, it is possible to be effective in proposing or even managing a change but a failure when it comes to delivering useful outcomes. The customer or user's satisfaction is the major indicator of effectiveness.

In the IT4B approach, *Effectiveness & Efficiency,* shown in context in Figure 3.3, is rooted in the decisions made regarding policy. If the governing council or board does not consider that efficiency is an issue then, regardless of strategic activities, the capability to be effective and efficient will not be addressed. *Objectives & Requirements* in the Strategy domain will not be predicated on policies that do not exist.

Developments & Trends and *Opportunities & Risks* are both dependent on the outcomes required by policy, so the overall effectiveness of the enterprise must also be predicated on the set outcomes.

Effectiveness versus efficiency

Whereas efficiency refers to how well something is done, effectiveness refers to how useful something is. A plane is a very effective form of transportation, able to move people across long distances to specific places, but it may be considered inefficient because of how it uses fuel.

Effectiveness is about doing the right task, whereas efficiency is about doing things in an optimal way, for example, doing it in the quickest or in the least expensive way. It could be the wrong thing to do, of course, but at least it was done optimally, which should make you feel better.

Productivity implies effectiveness and efficiency in individual and enterprise performance. Effectiveness, then, is also the achievement of the objectives/requirements in the IT4B model. Efficiency is the achievement of the ends using the minimum amount of resources and activities (also illustrated in the model). All public-sector enterprises are under pressure to perform. The private sector is always under pressure from Wall Street or shareholders. Recent government initiatives have focused on the need for all public-sector bodies to deliver greater efficiency, to ensure that the most effective results are obtained from available resources. Many change programmes in the public sector will continue to be concerned primarily with improving performance.

In many cases, the enterprise will have specific performance targets set, and programmes of radical change may be required to achieve those targets. These programmes will need to pay particular attention to the *Review & Validation* capabilities/activities and to the evaluation of outcomes. The enterprise will want to establish that the target performance levels have been achieved, but some thought should also be given to establishing the role of the change programme in meeting the objectives.

In complex programmes of organisational change, it can be difficult or even impossible to establish, after the event, that specific activities or policies in the change programme gave rise to identifiable and quantifiable improvements. Chains of cause and effect must be carefully considered in planning the change, and monitored during implementation. The approach to measurement of performance improvements and other objectives must be considered as part of the planning of the change programme, and not tacked on later as an afterthought. *Review & Validation* is an activity in the model to ensure that objectives and requirements as described in the improvement (the change) are being fully developed. These improvements must have the desired impact when in operation, and are an indicator of effectiveness and efficiency.

Effectiveness and efficiency in the real world

Let's use a service desk as an example to discuss effectiveness and efficiency. A commonly used example of effectiveness is the 'ITIL compliant' service desk, where some genius decided that the best measures of effectiveness involved the speed by which a phone call was answered. For example, was the telephone answered quickly (e.g. 90% of the calls answered within X seconds)? This led to quick fixes and repeated calls because no one did anything more than try to meet the target of answering a call. Who cared if the answer was correct?

Is the service restored within an acceptable time and in accordance with the service level agreement (SLA)? SLAs rarely reflected business need; IT relied upon a published 'ITIL' SLA template that applied to no one in particular and was used generically, resulting in very irritated business customers.

Are users advised in time about current and future changes and errors? What did 'in time' actually mean? The use of loose phraseology and generic SLAs resulted in poor service and outsourcing.

Some performance indicators can only be measured by means of a customer survey, e.g.:

- Is the telephone answered courteously?

- Are users given good advice on how to prevent incidents?

These sorts of questions were more open, but yet again somewhat loose in phrasing. Your good service is my unhelpful service desk.

Building a performance framework is necessary no matter what the focus of a performance management exercise, or overall effectiveness or efficiency of resolution. You may be seeking to assess the performance of a business unit, a small department, a team, a contract or an individual – the attributes of a good performance framework are the same regardless of scale or scope.

Setting up a framework is as much an art as a science. It may prove difficult to build the framework without knowledge of how it will work in practice, or how useful the information it produces will turn out to be. Learn from the experience of others where possible, and ensure that the framework itself, as well as the information it produces, is subject to evaluation and review.

Why measure performance?

Performance measures lie at the heart of demonstrating effectiveness and efficiency. They provide the first, vital link in a chain that leads to better services, improved business models and the realisation of outcomes. Measurements provide the foundations for improvement:

- You could be rewarding failure if you can't identify and reward success.
- What does success actually look like? And to whom? When you can't see success, you can't learn from it.
- If you can't recognise failure, you can't correct it.

- If you can demonstrate success, you can win support – from management, customers, and in the case of the public sector, the citizen.

It is a fact that what gets measured gets done; however, too much emphasis on performance measurement carries with it the risk that the measurement process becomes an end in itself. It is important not to lose sight of the fundamental objectives of performance measurement. Think about how many enterprises spent a fortune implementing an IT method such as ITIL; they implemented ITIL but did not identify any business benefits that meant anything to anyone outside of IT.

Management reports

A useful and effective tool is the good old management report. Avoid stupid advice that suggests reporting myriad issues and even more stupid advice about 'exception' reports. Find out what business people want, or what IT management wants to see. Do not just copy the templates of an enterprise that has absolutely nothing in common with yours. IT4B stresses the importance of reporting against the requirements of a benefits model.

The 'output' or the 'outcome'?

In the Governance quadrant it is clear that the root is Outcome; benefits to the business or public-sector body that may even be tangential to some activities. Tracking benefits is the only means of demonstrating gain, which in turn points to effective performance management and effective measurement to enable benefits to be recognised.

Output is largely not an issue in Governance (no one is likely to care if the output is a service, a product or an app, or if it is built in-house or externally); digital transformation will be the Governance issue, but the executive focus is never going to be on the specifics of IT. This also means that the focus on technology will be somewhat less than perfunctory; someone will throw in a few buzzwords but the lead will be taken by the senior responsible owner (SRO) of any programme (or by their proxy). The board or governing council has little time to even think about data as an asset. Governance with regard to digital transformation means defining the mission for the future. If that is considered 'the output', so be it. The mission summarises the desired future for the enterprise; it expresses 'where we want to be' in relation to the enterprise's business success. It indicates the areas of significant change and the desired outcome of improvements and developments.

Opportunities & Risks

Governance

- Translate new developments and trends into new value propositions and benefit models
- Assess new developments and trends for possible impact on the enterprise

 ... from a business service perspective
 ... from an information service perspective
 ... from an application service perspective
 ... from a technology service perspective

Opportunities & Risks

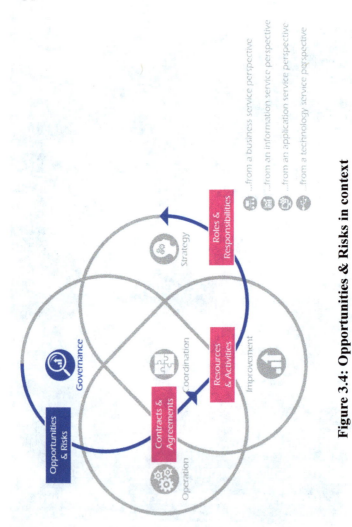

...from a business service perspective

...from an information service perspective

...from an application service perspective

...from a technology service perspective

Strategy

Governance

Roles & Responsibilities

Coordination

Resources & Activities

Improvement

Opportunities & Risks

Contracts & Agreements

Operation

Figure 3.4: Opportunities & Risks in context

The translation of new developments and trends into new value propositions and benefit models is key in assessing *Opportunities & Risks*. *Developments & Trends* and *Opportunities & Risks* form the balance of true innovation. What is expected is realistic innovation: to be open minded about business and technology opportunities balanced by a healthy risk assessment.

Why reinvent the wheel? Let's recap sound advice about managing risk and managing opportunity.

Risk

Risk can be defined as uncertainty of outcome, whether positive opportunity or negative threat. The term 'management of risk' incorporates all the activities required to identify and control the exposure to risk, which may have an impact on the achievement of enterprise business objectives. For a 'definitive definition' of risk, consult ISO standards.

Every enterprise manages its risk, but not always in a way that is visible, repeatable and consistently applied to support decision making. The task of management of risk is to ensure that the enterprise makes cost-effective use of a risk process that has a series of well-defined steps. The aim is to support better decision making through a good understanding of risks and their likely impact.

There are two distinct phases: risk analysis and risk management. Risk analysis is concerned with gathering information about exposure to risk so that the enterprise can make appropriate decisions and manage risk appropriately.

Risk management involves having processes in place to monitor risks, access to reliable and up-to-date information about risks, the right balance of control in place to deal with those risks, and decision-making processes supported by a framework of risk analysis and evaluation.

Risk management covers a wide range of topics, including business continuity management, security, programme/project risk management and operational service management. These topics need to be placed in the context of an organisational framework for the management of risk. Some risk-related topics, such as security, are highly specialised and this guidance provides only an overview.

Why risk management is important

A certain amount of risk taking is inevitable if your enterprise is to achieve its objectives. Effective risk management helps you to improve efficiency by contributing to:

- Increased certainty and fewer surprises;
- Better service delivery;
- More effective change management;
- More efficient use of resources;
- Better management at all levels through improved decision making; and
- Reduced waste and fraud, and better value for money.

Opportunity

Without taking risks, many businesses would long ago have gone out of business. Risk taking is perfectly reasonable in both business and government enterprises if the opportunity for improvement in services or revenues is worthwhile and if the risks are reasonable or perhaps can be managed or even avoided.

Uber, for example, knew the risk that many governments would legislate against their business; however, the risks were manageable and the profits would be worthwhile.

Asset stripping can be legal and risk free or you can try to hide your ill-gotten gains in the Cayman Islands. Morality aside, the only issue is the risk that the individual or corporation wishes to take. Ask Starbucks or Google if they assessed risk before taking the opportunity to avoid taxation. If we owe the government a few hundred in taxes, canines are loosed upon us; if you owe billions then a few nasty words in a press release seems to be the only risk.

Channels

In the public sector, recent policy was for service delivery to be 'citizen-centred', taking government to the customer (or business) and adapting the services to their requirements rather than requiring them to interact on government terms; further, it was policy for government as a purchaser to conduct its business electronically with its providers.

In the area of channel policy, this may mean offering a single service *via* multiple channels – continuing to offer it *via* a traditional channel while also providing the option to use a newer channel. In the private sector, the situation was widely available, where companies have opened a range of channels to sell their products and deliver their services, tailoring their approaches to the preferences of their customers. The channels were created to save money; make something look like providing 'opportunity' by appearing to provide choice, and someone will think that 'do it yourself travel booking' is saving them time and money, whereas the reality is that they are spending hours behind a computer screen doing all the work that was once done for them and saving travel companies a stack of cash.

3: The 'roman riding' of governance

Some examples of services available online (and through other channels) in various areas of the private sector:

- Travel: most people can book a holiday entirely online.
- Financial services: product comparisons (of mortgages, insurance and investment products, for example), or the opportunity to trade shares and lose money without blaming the agent.
- Predictions of investment growth.
- Retail opportunities:
  - A combination of physical retail space, mail order and online ordering channels.
  - The weekly shopping ordered online can be delivered at a time and location convenient to the customer.
- Price comparison sites to help people find retailers or services, such as plumbers or electricians.

Services are often grouped in ways that are useful to the customer. Commercial websites often provide a gateway or 'portal' to related services. Government Internet portals, such as www.ukonline.gov.uk and the planning services portal www.planningportal.co.uk, are good examples.

Most local authorities have a range of service delivery options with e-service facilities. Many of these include a contact centre, with web-enabled information and transaction services. Central government examples include the Inland Revenue self-assessment and submission of returns services; Ordnance Survey's range of services to other public-sector enterprises and to customers is another.

Research suggested that digital television was likely to be the main channel for delivering e-service to those who couldn't afford to (or preferred not to) own and run a computer

3: The 'roman riding' of governance

connected to the Internet. Guess why digital television became popular.

In summary: take a risk here and there, but be sure it has been assessed.

Strategy

Sourcing &
Sponsoring

Architecture
& Portfolio

Objectives &
Requirements

Roles &
Responsibilities

 ... from a business service perspective

 ... from an information service perspective

 ... from an application service perspective

 ... from a technology service perspective

CHAPTER FOUR: THE EQUILIBRIUM OF STRATEGY

How to keep resilience and agility in balance?

The dynamics of strategy and IT

Strategy is the means by which equilibrium is reached between the opposing dynamics 'How to be both resilient *and* agile and how to maintain the status quo while attempting to adapt to new challenges (business, information/data, applications/services and technology)' – usually through investing in innovative business or IT practices or technologies. The strategic themes described at governance/board level must now be translated into an action plan.

Following deliberations in Governance, the policy outcomes, stakeholder needs and risks associated with the preferred option for improvement are key inputs to this activity. From the business perspective, the strategy for using technology has to be focused on automating business processes for efficiency (perhaps radically) and ensuring that the business strategy for the digital enterprise is reflected in the IT strategy. As we described earlier with regard to the camera obscura, there is an analogy between the modern exploitation of technology to achieve business goals with the example from the Middle Ages.

Key areas

The key areas for delivery planning are:

- Policy deliverables, including how each will be achieved – with what resources and against what timetable of activities;
- Communications, tailored to the stakeholder audience;
- Risks, assessed by probability and impact, and supported by proposals for risk management;
- Resource planning, reflecting known or estimated requirements of the time, staff skills and numbers, necessary infrastructure and budgets; and
- Accountabilities, summarising who is responsible for doing what, by when and to what standard, under the project and programme structures described. How will progress be reported and monitored?

Gateway guidance

For those familiar with UK and Dutch government policy regarding Gateway reviews, it is recommended that on completion of delivery planning a 'Gate 0' review should be conducted. Gateway 0 focuses on the programme or project business justification. It also provides assurance to the programme or project board that the business requirement has been adequately researched and fits within the department's overall business strategy. Used at programme level, the review will, in addition, examine how the planned portfolio of projects aims to deliver the overall programme objectives, and that the programme management structure, monitoring and resourcing is appropriate. This review tests the robustness of selected options. It checks the coherence, consistency and completeness of delivery preparations and planning, especially where accountabilities might have been dispersed among a number of individuals. This is in effect a Gateway where a go/no go decision is taken and is an essential review point, especially where delivery planning tasks have been delegated to a number of individuals.

From the above you can see that Gateway requires goal setting to be a crucial activity. It should also be clear that using the IT4B approach will assist with goal setting and aligning those goals with Operation.

Effective delivery requires that interdependencies are managed effectively. Interdependencies can occur anywhere: between programmes, projects or individual deliverables. They are often complex and dynamic, so need to be assessed and managed as an ongoing process.

Outcome and output

Creating a strategy means clarifying, creating and refining the strategic vision, strategic issues, strategic themes and the candidate programmes and/or projects that will go forward with approval. The business outcomes are the focus, though attention must be paid to the outputs that would be likely because leaving these issues to Improvement would be leaving things late and inviting scope creep and cost. The strategic vision expresses the putative future for the enterprise, its desired position in relation to its partner and supply chain ecosystem (*Sourcing & Sponsoring*) and the outcomes it wishes to bring about, both within the enterprise and in its dealings with customers and information chain partners. Be aware that an outcome is not the same as an output. An IT service may be a delivered output but if it does not achieve what it was intended, it has a failed outcome.

The strategic vision can be seen as a blueprint for improvement. It might well focus on a number of related (and sometimes unrelated) changes that are managed in the Improvement domain and should be fundamentally focused on outcomes, which are set in policies defined in Governance. Outcomes are the changes the enterprise or line of business (LoB) aims to make to improve the benefits for the good of the enterprise and/or its customers or partners. Government examples might include a healthier population, improved access to education, a reduction in crime or a reduction in the cost of public administration. Information services will be essential in each of these themes: collection and distribution of healthcare information (which will be subject to privacy regulations), creation of accessible websites and distribution of information, and collection of financial data for action. Such issues are described in IT4B as *Objectives & Requirements*. Keep in mind that we are not trying to reinvent IT; by using the IT4B model and its nomenclature, the idea is to place crucial and sometimes complex elements in a context that enables understanding, recognition, rapid navigation and assessment. The issues we have found to be most common are shown in Figure 4.1.

In essence, describing the strategy and its objectives and requirements provides a roadmap for improvement. It should be clear that the functional elements of *Architecture & Portfolio* are the pivotal components to ensure that improvements are delivered that accord with both outcomes and outputs.

An enterprise-wide information services strategy can be defined as comprising the information, business information services and most of the technology elements of the enterprise business. Imperatives, constraints and policies will be set by Governance and will require compliance *(Policy & Compliance)*, and Strategy will set metrics that will demonstrate achievement.

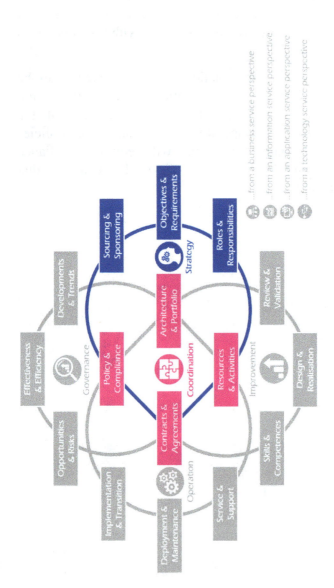

Figure 4.1: Touchstone elements and Strategy

In the gyroscope, the central tenet of Strategy, *Architecture & Portfolio*, is focused on enterprise growth through a twin focus on *Roles & Responsibilities* and *Sourcing & Sponsoring*. In turn, these activities contribute to the overall *Objectives & Requirements* of the enterprise by fulfilling the business mission. *Architecture & Portfolio* is a product of the activities initiated in the Governance domain. A direction will need to be established that assesses *Sourcing & Sponsoring* options and architectural capabilities based on *Roles & Responsibilities*.

Figure 4.1 illustrates that the essential outcome of Strategy is *Objectives & Requirements* as part of the process of ensuring outcomes (and to a greater extent than is present in the Governance domain, outputs, i.e. improvements).

RFCs, that arose from *Need and Value*, and which were analysed in *Developments & Trends*), will also provide specific outputs and outcomes.

Necessary strategic developments will be in line with the business mission and will almost certainly require a reassessment of the enterprise capabilities. The pivotal role of *Architecture & Portfolio* in the centre of the Strategy domain cannot be underestimated. It will be necessary to establish a means of demonstrating compliance with policy directives.

Policies will by necessity impact enterprise *Architecture & Portfolio* in the Strategy domain and how *Objectives & Requirements* are taken forward in the development of improvement activities. The services resulting from developing new or improved digital services might well be subject to contractual agreements; contracts with external parties will be established at board level and the issue of compliance will be central.

Architecture & Portfolio

Strategy

- Design and maintain the complex or structure of the enterprise
- Monitor the range of projects and developments and their impact on the enterprise

 ... from a business service perspective

 ... from an information service perspective

 ... from an application service perspective

 ... from a technology service perspective

Architecture & Portfolio

In Figure 4.1 we illustrate the central position of *Architecture & Portfolio* and the outcomes as defined in *Objectives & Requirements*; as discussed previously, without solid plans based on widely understood objectives for both outputs and expected outcomes, Strategy is worthless.

In most enterprises, each LoB will need to develop a digital information services strategy that supports its particular digital information needs within the information services framework defined enterprise wide. The strategy will most likely contain, inter alia, Finance, HR and business information elements. Generic information services such as libraries, a records centre or statistical services will depend on the enterprise; some will be provided by external parties, some by internal suppliers. The issue here is that each LoB might have identified *Developments & Trends* (or issues relating to *Effectiveness & Efficiency*) that require improvement to services, to technology, or even simply to the way the enterprise conducts business.

Strategies and the stages of strategy development

IT4B is important to ensure strategic themes are enacted as expected. Consider also interface changes, focusing on how the enterprise positions itself in relation to its business environment both internally and with partners in terms of how it will do business or how its business needs will be achieved (perhaps through new ways of working with suppliers and/or customers).

Although IT4B is not directly concerned with internal changes that focus on how the enterprise wishes to be constituted, such as any internal restructuring, infrastructure renewal or even change of culture, it must be influential in ensuring that such changes reflect the need to manage information with integrity and in line with governance.

Results that are strategic but represent only a stage along the path to achieving more significant outcomes are known as intermediate outcomes. In your enterprise, a programme directing the work of an employee training scheme might increase the number of employees trained to certain levels or in certain disciplines *(Skills & Competences,* one of which might be sales). For this scheme, an intermediate outcome might be a raised level of sales expertise in the workforce, and a final or policy outcome could be the beneficial effect on market share. Appendix D discusses a successful skills framework concept.

Strategic issues

An issue is a challenge facing the enterprise that requires action. It may be regarded as a problem or an opportunity. Issues that are critical to the enterprise's high-level plans for realising transformation outcomes, or that could jeopardise its business, are strategic issues.

All enterprises will differ in terms of the issues to which they must respond; there is no 'one size fits all'. The range of relevant issues will depend on individual circumstances, although many enterprises will identify common elements. There are the issues of *Roles & Responsibilities* that need to be identified (and in place) to enable improvements and, of course, to deliver outcomes and outputs as needed. Generally speaking, there are four categories of issue that will require someone, somewhere to play their role:

- Business – how the enterprise interacts with its customers, information chain partners and suppliers and supply chains, provides its digital services, and improves efficiency or revenue by meeting rising customer/citizen expectations.

- Political – decision-making, hierarchies, policy issues, rationalisation of services.
- Cultural – values, attitudes, competencies and relationships, such as the need to change the existing behaviour of staff and customers in order to work in new ways.
- Technical – IT, business information management and communication concerns, e.g. requirements for improved security on information provided and shared electronically, digital delivery, Cloud common standards for information exchange, interoperability. A critical success factor for a strategy is being able to demonstrate that a key issue has been addressed in a way that is clear and can be measured. *Opportunities & Risks* functions (or those charged with assessing opportunity and risk) will be responsible for identifying many of the critical success factors.

Roles & Responsibilities

Strategy

- Define the operating model and the key activities of the enterprise
- Assign the specific responsibilities to the relevant stakeholders

 ... from a business service perspective
 ... from an information service perspective
 ... from an application service perspective
 ... from a technology service perspective

Roles & Responsibilities

The contribution of *Roles & Responsibilities* in the activities of the Strategy domain is with regard to the focus on arriving at well thought-out *Objectives & Requirements*, without which we all may as well go home.

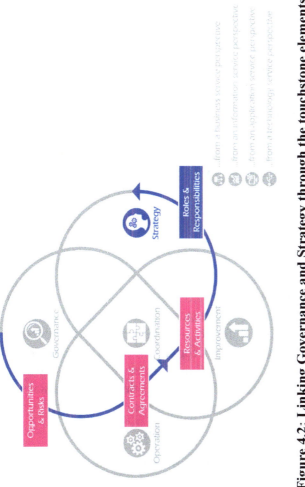

Figure 4.2: Linking Governance and Strategy through the touchstone elements

The essence of *Roles & Responsibilities* activities centres around the assignment of responsibilities to the relevant stakeholders (business, information, services/applications, technology). *Contracts & Agreements* and *Resources & Activities* activities will provide their input in preparation, as well as those involved with *Opportunities & Risks*. As shown in Figure 4.2, key touchstone elements come into play when *Roles & Responsibilities* are clear and provide a link between Governance and Strategy.

Roles & Responsibilities

Roles & Responsibilities is not always about the roles that are involved in evolving strategy. Together with *Architecture & Portfolio* it is also about the roles that are important in organising around the enterprise architecture – from strategic to operational, from business to technology.

In other domains, *Roles & Responsibilities* (and *Skills & Competences*) will also impact activities not directly related to Strategy.

Those involved in strategy formulation are senior management, the study team and the wider enterprise (business managers, customers who use the enterprise services and others with a stake in the successful outcome of the strategy, including service partners). The interests and concerns of the wider enterprise will be addressed during the study through focus groups, interviews and awareness briefings. The roles and responsibilities of both management and the study team are described below.

Senior management involvement

There must be senior management involvement, with the following roles clearly identified:

- The SRO: a 'champion' for the strategy.
- Beneficiaries who will gain from the strategy's implementation.
- 'Deliverers' – those who deliver the benefits from business improvement programmes.

Management's main concerns in relation to the strategy study are:

- To ensure that the evolving information services strategy is directly harnessed to business and policy objectives and priorities, data and information needs and innovative technologies;
- To review and approve the study's progress at designated checkpoints, and to approve the continuation of the study to the next stage; and
- To approve the formal deliverables of the study.

Subsequently, management's concerns will be:

- To ensure that implementation plans for business change are completed;
- To progress the strategy through strategic themes;
- To ensure that benefits are delivered and objectives met; and
- To ensure continuing compliance (*Policy & Compliance*) with business priorities.

In later stages, if options for information systems solutions are being investigated in detail, understanding of technology issues becomes important. Throughout, the team needs to be led by business-oriented managers who can ensure that the strategic emphasis is retained and continuity of the thinking process maintained.

Providers and partners

Many enterprises work closely with their providers or partners *(Sourcing & Sponsoring)* in developing strategy, especially where a long-term strategic relationship is in place. Examples can be seen in both the public and private sectors; the deciding factor is the level of involvement required. There may be reciprocal arrangements for attending board meetings, formulating strategy, reporting progress on strategic themes and taking action as part of ongoing strategic management.

Sourcing & Sponsoring covers both the issues of partnership (and managing suppliers) and the fiduciary issues relating to the programme or project that begin with the SRO and are executed throughout the programme.

The grouping of key roles (*Roles & Responsibilities*) and the relationship between the roles is fundamental to successful delivery. Where roles are combined (especially appropriate for smaller/less complex projects) it is important to ensure that delegating and reporting arrangements are understood by all involved. For example, consider project management.

Project management

Essential project management roles and responsibilities are:

- Investment decision-making – takes the investment decision based on affordability and cost justification (may be known as the investment decision maker (IDM), a key *Sourcing & Sponsoring* issue);
- Ownership – defines the scope and content of the project for delivering the benefits; personally accountable for the project's success (usually known as the SRO or project owner, as this role must be taken by a senior individual in the enterprise. The SRO/project owner

should have the status and authority to provide the necessary leadership and must have clear accountability for delivering the project outcome;

- Interface between ownership and delivery (sponsorship/directing) – ongoing management on behalf of the owner to ensure that the desired project objectives are delivered; must have adequate knowledge and information about the business and the project to be able to make informed decisions (may be known as the project sponsor; sometimes referred to as the project director);
- Project management – leading, managing and coordinating the project team on a day-to-day basis (the project manager); and
- Project team – delivers the required outputs or deliverables (the project team).

Objectives & Requirements

Strategy

- Address the strategic issues facing the enterprise
- Translate the strategic themes into obtainable goals
- Define requirements and constraints that will lead the enterprise in achieving those goals

 ... from a business service perspective

 ... from an information service perspective

 ... from an application service perspective

 ... from a technology service perspective

Objectives & Requirements

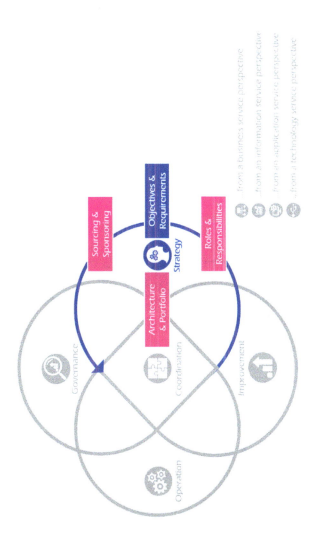

Figure 4.3: Positioning Objectives & Requirements as output

Since the strategic themes, if correctly identified, will address the strategic issues facing the enterprise, the realisation of the themes will lead the enterprise in the right direction (Figure 4.3). The vision for the future can be expressed in terms of the outcome of pursuing the themes of the strategy. The vision statement can be constructed by considering what the situation will be as a result of progressing each of the themes in the strategy. In this case, the vision statement will be produced after the themes have been defined and agreed with Governance. See Appendix B for some ideas about what questions to ask when formulating business and IT strategy.

Business case for the strategy

The business case for the strategy will be a justification for the strategy in business terms, taking into account, in broad terms, the financial implications as well as relevant qualitative issues. For example, it will seek to demonstrate that:

- The themes for the strategy have been correctly identified (that is, they are indeed 'strategic' for the enterprise, and there are no others that are more important);
- The strategy adequately addresses the issues confronting the enterprise (so far as these issues are amenable to business change as the way forward);
- The business assumptions on which the strategy is based are reasonable;
- The strategy adopts an acceptable position in relation to the risk and uncertainty with which it must deal;
- The benefits that will be derived from the realisation of the strategy are in line with wider business objectives;

- The strategy is realisable and politically acceptable (for example, to the stakeholders in the enterprise); and
- The mechanisms and procedures for monitoring and progressing the strategy within the enterprise will be effective.

The development of individual business cases for programmes and projects to realise the strategy will focus on the need to demonstrate business and strategic 'fit' with the business strategy's overall direction.

It is unlikely that the business case for the strategy will be supported by detailed financial analysis. It may not be meaningful to assess the 'value for money of the strategy' since there will not always be detailed information about money in the strategy. The business case for the strategy provides a defined context for the individual business change initiatives through which the strategy will be progressed. A channel is a route through which services can be delivered. Examples of channels for service delivery include:

- Face-to-face interaction (information kiosks, home visits, etc.);
- Written interaction (by post, fax, etc.);
- Telephony (to call centres, for example);
- The Internet (e-business, electronic service delivery); and
- Digital television.

Most enterprises need to consider carefully how they can exploit new technologies *(Opportunities and Risks)*, to meet the needs of their customers. In most cases this will mean an assessment of how information within the enterprise can be delivered to or provided by the customer in new ways, or how the customer can interact with the enterprise in new ways – choosing new channels for service delivery.

The more 'traditional' channels (face-to-face or written communication) are likely to be in place already. The enterprise must decide whether it will offer innovative channels such as the Internet and digital television alongside, or even instead of, traditional channels.

Customer priorities

Customers will not accept changes that succeed only in moving the queue from a counter to a kiosk, or replacing a simple, familiar procedure with a confusing online experience. Nor will many customers seek out new channels simply because they are new. Customer priorities and concerns are likely to include:

- Quality of service
- Direct cost of service:
  - o Flat fee for subscription or unlimited use
  - o Charges
- Indirect costs:
  - o Phone calls
  - o Buying and running a computer
  - o Subscribing to TV service
- Accessibility (for the disabled, visually impaired, etc.)
- Ease of use, comprehensibility and clarity of presentation
- Availability and flexibility

In many cases it may be that what is most convenient for the enterprise is least convenient for the customer. In such cases, the enterprise will have to work hard to ensure that its service is accessible and easy to use. A customer concern (such as usability) may be hard to reconcile with an organisational concern (such as development cost). The customer's concern should take priority as far as possible. It seems likely that there will always be a need for a physical presence, particularly for more complex services.

New channels and e-services should be developed with customers if they are to be successful. Holding user groups as part of the development process is a good step towards involving customers at the earliest possible stage.

Managing the relationship with the customer

Managing the relationship with the customer is all about managing the effectiveness of every customer interaction – maximising opportunities for service improvement, capturing requirements and feedback for use throughout the enterprise and strengthening the customer relationship at every opportunity. This requires far more than just an enterprise-wide customer database; it often means changing the organisational structure and underlying business processes.

New self-service channels can open up new services, increase customer satisfaction and improve efficiency. But meeting the expectations of customers can be problematic. Customers are demanding more channels, yet the investments required are so expensive that even the largest enterprises may be hard-pressed to invest in every channel. There is the risk of an excess of innovative ideas. What is needed is a single, clearly articulated vision for an enterprise's relationship with the customer so that the various efforts can be more productive and less confusing.

Change must be based on evaluating the benefits to customers and solutions found that are cost-effective for customers as well as for the enterprise providing the service.

E-business

E-business is the provision of information, services and transactions through electronic media. This often, though not always, means providing them through a browser interface so that they can be accessed by anyone with access to the Internet.

E-business in the public sector is often referred to as electronic service delivery: any service delivered electronically to customers, which could include two-way information exchange and transactions. E-business plays a key role in improving services to the public and making it easier for the customer to interact with government at all levels.

New developments in infrastructure will make electronic service delivery much easier to achieve, especially when collaborating across organisational boundaries. The Government Secure Intranet is one example in the public sector; another is the National Grid for Learning, linking educational establishments and service providers nationwide. The National Land Information Service brings Ordnance Survey, Land Registry, the Valuation Office Agency and local authorities together to provide a service for those seeking information about a property.

E-business also covers innovations that are of benefit to the enterprise in the way it does business internally, or with its partners, such as intranets and e-procurement.

Benefits

E-business services can realise benefits for both the customer who uses them and the enterprise that provides them.

For the customer:

- Reducing time taken queuing or waiting
- More information found, quicker
- Speeding up financial transactions
- Empowerment: convenience, ease of access, flexibility in options and hours of service

For the enterprise:

- Simplifying procedures and documentation
- Improving accuracy
- Lower staff turnover
- Reduced need for workspace dedicated to face-to-face contact with customers
- Eliminating interactions that do not yield outcomes
- Extending contact opportunities beyond office hours where there is a demand
- Improving relationships with customers through better customer service
- Enabling information to be used more effectively, creating more complex, rich and rounded knowledge resources
- Improving the image of the enterprise and government as a whole

Problems

Technology can resolve service delivery problems but may actually create new problems unless appropriate policies are in place to ensure the benefits achieved are available to all. E-business also brings the potential for problems including:

- Over-optimism about e-business capabilities;
- Repeated failures to learn from past mistakes;
- Initiatives that are not thought through and/or poorly coordinated;

- Lack of focus on customer needs; and
- Failure to address the needs of those who cannot (or do not want to) use e-services.

Sourcing & Sponsoring

Strategy

- Establish whether the strategic objectives can be achieved with the available competences and resources of the enterprise
- Establish whether additional competences and resources are required
- Ensure the allocation of all required competences and resources

 ... from a business service perspective

 ... from an information service perspective

 ... from an application service perspective

 ... from a technology service perspective

Sourcing & Sponsoring

In this part of the discussion about agile versus resilience, and how to deal with challenges, we will consider *Sourcing & Sponsoring* in more detail. Figure 4.4 illustrates the primary activities that inform *Sourcing & Sponsoring*, with perhaps the most important being the politics of the enterprise.

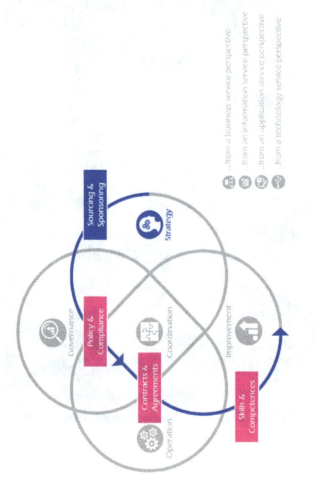

Figure 4.4. Sourcing & Sponsoring

The activities are part of the Strategy domain, so together with getting the objectives and the requirements straight, it's all about knowing the context (*Architecture & Portfolio*) and knowing the enterprise around the enterprise architecture (*Roles & Responsibilities*). *Sourcing & Sponsoring* is all about establishing digital readiness. Will we achieve the objectives of the enterprise with the components and people that the enterprise already has? If we cannot, this is a measure of digital (un)readiness.

What do we have to do to make that right?

Will we have to make, buy or ally with regard to missing components?

Will we have to develop the re-required *Skills & Competences*?

Or do we partner with external professionals?

Sourcing & Sponsoring takes the role to define a sourcing strategy and provide sponsorship and commissioning for the proposed improvement (business, information, applications/services, technology). *Policy & Compliance* validates the proposed improvement, and *Contracts & Agreements* ensures both internal and external commitment.

Sourcing & Sponsoring is all about ensuring that the strategy for digital services can be executed. The outputs from the activities should lead to clearly defined *Objectives & Requirements* and clearly defined outputs and outcomes based on easily identifiable measurable benefits. The IT4B digital profile is a starting point of communications for planning and sourcing activities. The activities, outputs, outcomes and benefits should be communicated across the enterprise. Planning how information about the instantiation of sourcing policy initiatives will be disseminated to stakeholders – the people directly involved in the policy development – to the people working in the enterprise, and to any other external enterprises is a key factor in ensuring successful delivery. One way of achieving this is to develop a communication strategy that defines how people will be able to feed back their views, issues and ideas.

When considering your communication strategy, you will need to think about the type of communication that will be required for each of the stakeholder groups. The stakeholder groups may be internal or external, they may be LoB groups, or they may even be government bodies. See Appendix C.

Improvement

Resources & Activities

Skills & Competences

Review & Validation

Design & Realisation

 ... from a business service perspective

 ... from an information service perspective

 ... from an application service perspective

 ... from a technology service perspective

CHAPTER FIVE: THE OUTER LIMITS OF IMPROVEMENT

> "That's been one of my mantras – focus and simplicity. Simple can be harder than complex: you have to work hard to get your thinking clean to make it simple. But it's worth it in the end, because once you get there, you can move mountains"
>
> **Steve Jobs**

Simplicity over complexity

What could possibly go wrong by improving?

Many IT-related projects are initiated to add some kind of new service to the application landscape. As a result, the enterprise architecture becomes more and more complex after each project. In many cases, commercial off-the-shelf software is acquired to meet specific needs of the enterprise. That standard software component likely has much more functionality than is needed (and used) at that particular time. This is often overlooked when 'the next project' emerges to meet some other need, resulting in an application landscape that is characterised by lots of overlapping services, both used and unused.

Improvement and IT

IT4B promotes a *reuse-reduce-recycle* approach to improvement projects rather than *grow-expand-explode*. Every project can either be seen as an opportunity to reduce the complexity of the existing business and IT architecture, or as a chance to (re)use services that are already available. This implies the existence of an inventory of all available services within the enterprise architecture.

So the question in Improvement is how to keep improving while retaining a well-balanced enterprise architecture.

Output or outcome?

Both, in more or less equal proportions, apply in this domain. Figure 6.2 illustrates that the essential element of Improvement is *Design & Realisation* in the process of validating strategic outcomes and therefore, to a large extent, the needed outputs, i.e. specific improvements, products or services, that were themselves initiated from *Need & Value*, and most likely followed some form of analysis of *Developments & Trends*.

Most design techniques (modern and traditional) distinguish between logical and physical design, even where Agile methods are the most widely employed. *Design & Realisation* should be leading the thinking irrespective of what architectural models or methods (*Skills & Competences*, e.g. TOGAF) are in use in the enterprise. Though terms may be different, TOGAF models are essentially no different in concept to older methods. Logical design is what you want an application or digital service to do, and physical design is how the application will comply with logical design. Logical design is, in turn, based on a

Master Data Model (MDM)/enterprise data model and cannot 'create' new entities.

Physical design has practical considerations such as operational efficiency (for example, a decision about what data should be used as a key for accessing physical records). An MDM is not a substitute for physical design; physical design is centred on obtaining a workable solution that performs in compliance with an acceptable set of criteria. Agreed requirements must serve the needs of the users of the information services; keep in mind that users will sometimes be customers, at other times they may be on the receiving end of what has been procured.

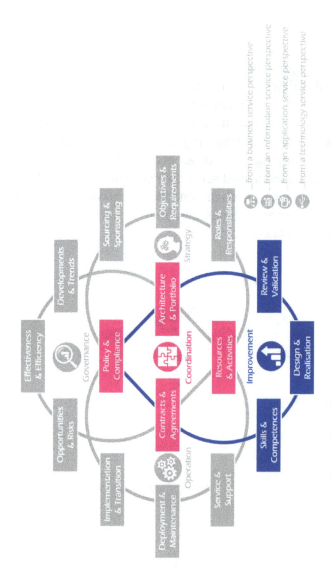

Figure 5.1: Touchstone elements and improvement

The influence of the touchstone activities is at the heart of all improvement discussions (Figure 5.1) because of the enormous impact on Operation. Improvement might well have been initiated in Operation (because of business needs or recognition of perhaps poorly designed digital services), though the shaping mechanism was through Governance and the decisions made regarding architecture, sourcing and building took place in strategic discussion.

In the gyroscope, the central tenet of improvement, *Resources & Activities*, is focused on enterprise improvement through a twin focus on *appropriate Skills & Competences* and *Review & Validation* of new or improved products/digital services. In turn, these activities contribute to the overall *Design & Realisation of digital services for* the enterprise that fulfil the business mission. Necessary developments will inevitably impact the business mission and will almost certainly require a reassessment of the enterprise capabilities. The pivotal role of *Policy & Compliance* in the centre of the Governance domain and that of *Architecture & Portfolio* in the Strategy domain cannot be underestimated. It will be necessary to establish a means of ensuring (and proving) compliance; new or improved digital services must meet the requirements set in strategy that are linked to governance directives.

Policies will by necessity impact enterprise *Architecture & Portfolio* in the Strategy domain and how objectives and requirements are taken forward in development of Improvement activities. The services resulting from developing new or improved digital services might well be subject to contractual agreements; contracts with external parties will have been established at board level.

Resources & Activities

Improvement

- Plan the availability of all required competences and resources
- Prevent that the use of resources exceeds the budget
- Schedule all required activities
- Ensure that activities are performed as planned

 ... from a business service perspective

 ... from an information service perspective

 ... from an application service perspective

 ... from a technology service perspective

Resources & Activities

The output is the *Design & Realisation* of the strategy to deliver new or improved digital services. And the design is subject to activities related not only to availability of resources but also contractual arrangements, policies and architecture.

What is the purpose of Improvement? It is to improve the use of the digital services or to improve 'the customer experience' of using digital services.

Someone has a responsibility to maintain the position of the business use of the information services throughout and should be responsible for overall quality of the delivery. *Resources & Activities* should be clearly the pivotal role (in turn dependent on available competences and capabilities, which would be identified in *Skills & Competences*).

To improve is to change; to be perfect is to change often.

– Winston Churchill

Digital service requirements

Once requirements have been defined and approved through *Objectives & Requirements*, it is possible to focus on the issues of what is or is not to be digitised. As indicated throughout, in the modern enterprise this is increasingly a decision that states electronic first and foremost, but which must be nuanced by being certain of what the customer or user will both need and value.

Examples would be that a charitable enterprise for the profoundly deaf might be able to 'go electronic', whereas one for the blind would be wise to consider audio as the delivery mechanism as well as catering for the partially sighted by enabling large-scale magnification. Who takes responsibility for these issues? Without IT4B focus on resources, activities, skills and competences, services will be inadequately designed and realised.

Electronic delivery of vital information for immigrant groups having no access to electronic instruments and no other language but their own might also be something of a failure.

Consider again the issue of language. Without IT4B as a central and effective discipline, service design of digital services becomes dependent on technologists who may not know all they need to know about customers, users and partners.

Design of the digital service

IT service design that has been taken forward from executive-level sessions (the stakeholder requirements) is most likely to meet resource constraints (people, time, money). Time spent agreeing the 'design of the design' will result in a design description that you will take forward into the development of a service. *Objectives & Requirements* and *Roles & Responsibilities* are key functions; these are not exclusive to others. *Sourcing & Sponsoring* might loom large as an issue. Improving and innovating IT-intensive service design will require a high-level exploration with stakeholders to arrive at a service design architecture (not a TOGAF architecture). Success depends on whether all the information is available to cover all the information requirements in the design and development stages. From a business point of view, you should have all the business information needs to justify further investment and sign-off.

Assembly

Build or buy is really the crux of design in the context of improving services (*Sourcing & Sponsoring*). Is the LoB free to buy from any source? What resources are available? Is the design one of complexity requiring either or both disciplines of programme and project management? Depending on the scale of the improvement or just the cost, a business case might be required and it should describe benefits and KPIs.

Assembling resources requires knowledge of information design requirements. Any change to an existing service should improve the service; if not there is no need because it has no value. The design approach will be similar irrespective of whether the information service (as a whole or in part) is being provided in-house or contracted out to a supplier; in the latter case a formal contract will be required.

Successful *Design & Realisation* of development planning depends on using suitably qualified personnel equipped with adequate resources. Similarly, the organisational and technical interfaces need to be defined (including those with customers and suppliers). These are likely to include ITIL/ASL processes such as service level management, capacity management, availability management, computer operations management, network services management, service/help desks, change management, incident and problem management, and the various personnel charged with managing and maintaining databases and related repositories and, of course, with hardware and software suppliers. Service design and development planning must allow for service level reporting. This is addressed by service level management.

Service *Review & Validation*

The digital service design should be validated against the following criteria:

- Consistency with the customer requirements.
- Completeness of the service delivery process.
- Availability of resources to meet the service obligations.
- Compliance with/conformance to any applicable standards or codes of practice.
- Availability of information to customers in the use of the service.

Agility in development of digital services is often thrown into the mix and the usual argument is that a process focus is too slow, outdated and not very Agile. Generally speaking, that sort of thinking is twaddle, as is the thinking that the process focus is the only way to be effective. Prototyping information services might well allow service delivery and deployment to proceed more quickly, but it might not help to achieve enterprise programme goals and outcomes and it might cause a lot of rework because dependencies may not be recognised. We say 'might' because all enterprises differ and accelerated development in an enterprise with only a single LoB might be more efficient than using a project management method that is designed to manage a more expansive canvas.

Maintain your stakeholder perspectives on IT

At this stage of digital information services development consider the integrity of the information service processing so that you can be certain that the service will be compliant with stakeholder needs, executive policies and LoB use. If the service is not focused on these criteria, it has no value and likely was not needed.

5: The outer limits of improvement

When it comes down to investing in the future by improving digital services (or perhaps replacing 'traditional' services), one question is always how to keep improving while retaining a well-balanced enterprise architecture.

Skills & Competences

Improvement

- Ensure the availability of the required skills and competences
- Develop or acquire any nescessary skill or competence that is lacking

 ... from a business service perspective

 ... from an information service perspective

 ... from an application service perspective

 ... from a technology service perspective

Skills & Competences

Let's look at the organisational tension surrounding Skills & Competences, which arises because of the need to have the right people, with the right skills, at the right time (Resources & Activities) in place to realise the focus on Design & Realisation of the strategic services. In tandem with Review & Validation, Skills & Competences work to realise the strategic vision.

The essential role of *Skills & Competences* (Figure 5.2) is to ensure that the required skills (and therefore capabilities) are either developed or acquired in all four (business, information, applications/services, technology) areas needed for digital transformation. Proposals will require the approval of those responsible for *Policy & Compliance* and *Contracts & Agreements*, as well as to some extent people involved with *Sourcing & Sponsoring*. The corollary is that people in the roles that enact each of those touchstone elements absolutely must have the necessary skills.

By looking at the portfolio of components, enterprise resource planning can identify the skills and qualifications needed for success. Skilled resources will then become available 'in the pool' for placement into programmes or projects or for related work. The function responsible for human resource management also needs to address organisational and resource impacts of major changes resulting from portfolio components.

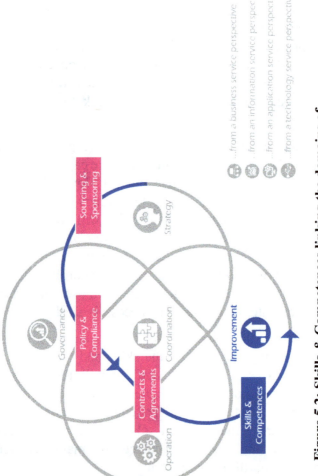

...from a business service perspective

...from an information service perspective

...from an application service perspective

...from a technology service perspective

Figure 5.2: Skills & Competences linking the domains of Governance, Strategy and Improvement

Understanding capabilities

Experience of major improvement initiatives indicates that a realistic understanding of your enterprise capabilities is a major factor for success; conversely, where skills and experience have not been considered the risks of failure are high. We strongly advise you to carry out a skills audit of your team before any improvement initiative gets underway and monitor the skills profile throughout the initiative (because operational situations dictate that team members often have to be deployed elsewhere). This will help you identify any areas of weakness and make contingency plans to address them.

Design & Realisation

Improvement

- Ensure that the design of the new product or service meets the strategic objectives of the enterprise
- Ensure that the realisation of the new product or service is accordingly to the design

 ... from a business service perspective

 ... from an information service perspective

 ... from an application service perspective

 ... from a technology service perspective

Design & Realisation

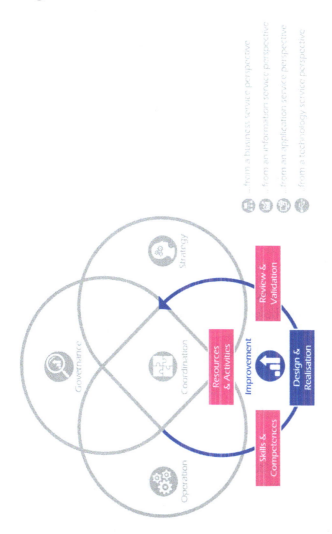

Figure 5.3: Design & Realisation as the output of Improvement

The *Design & Realisation* processes (Figure 5.3) in an enterprise result in the definition and maintenance of the enterprise architecture, applications (services) architecture and the IT infrastructure. These processes cover all aspects of IT, including roles and responsibilities, and also provide coordination with data design and service management processes.

Design & Realisation is the ultimate output of the Improvement domain, including the touchstone element *Resources & Activities, Review & Validation* and *Skills & Competences*. The focus is on improving the business, applications (digital information services) and technologies.

Together, design and realisation processes align the diverse requirements and preferences related to both applications and the IT infrastructure, including:

- Transformative work for digital service;
- Balancing the business requirements with the costs of IT services;
- Striking a balance between the risks and costs of innovation and the resulting competitive advantage;
- Interfacing with the infrastructure of partner enterprises;
- Complying with relevant standards;
- Coordination between IT planners and business planners; and
- Tactical control of all projects, in conjunction with service management and other disciplines.

Many strategies and projects fail because of a lack of planning and a failure to monitor the implementation of the associated plans. The *Design & Realisation* processes should ensure that all those concerned are adequately informed of the strategy, policy and plans. To provide effective coordination with the business operations of the enterprise we advise setting up a steering group, which includes both business and IT managers, and which meets regularly to discuss the feasibility and progress of the strategic and tactical project plans.

A good management system uses people, processes and resources effectively and efficiently. Effective control requires that the links between these three aspects are transparent. The decision process is largely dependent on the information and reports provided by the processes. In turn, the processes depend on the deployment of personnel and IT tools to provide management information. The management system should be able to integrate information from a range of technical management domains.

The management process is based on a recurring cycle:

- Reviewing the current position, including processes, policy and external factors.
- Defining the target state, which should result in compliance with mission, strategy, policy and objectives.
- Designing and implementing the plans to migrate to the target state, including results and performance indicators, followed by their implementation in projects. Plans will include:
  - The IT services and their quality;
  - Personnel, skills and training levels;
  - Processes, policy and procedures;
  - All documentation aspects;
  - Geographical aspects such as locations and environments; and
  - External factors such as market trends and developments.

The project is defined in concrete terms with measurable targets, allocated budgets, KPIs and critical success factors.

Designing and implementing the plans

Designing and implementing the plans is a demanding activity with all the hallmarks of a carefully implemented programme or project. The elements include:

- Creating an IT group that can ensure the successful implementation of the strategy;
- Creating support for the strategy outside the IT enterprise;
- Obtaining budgets and resources for successful implementation;
- Developing processes and procedures to support the strategy to improve or build the digital services;
- Creating a supportive working environment and culture;
- Ensuring adequate leadership and the commitment and support of the entire IT management;
- Integrating the improvements in the routine operations of all personnel;
- Phasing out processes and structures that are incompatible with the strategy;
- Implementing best practices and improvement programmes; and
- Reviewing and evaluating the plan's progress.

Progress monitoring is a continual activity, which may use a balanced score card or other instruments. All IT managers are responsible for monitoring and evaluating progress by:

- Evaluating the performance of the IT enterprise;
- Evaluating the performance of the teams;
- Evaluating personal performance;

- Assessing external developments; and
- Obtaining external feedback and acting on it.

Design phase

In the design phase we also have to consider existing common infrastructure services, such as network services, naming services, directory services, communication services, database services, middleware, APIs, etc. The intention is that further development is compatible with the *de facto* standards typically based upon key suppliers' products. This requires information about the design of the IT infrastructure, which means that an adequate configuration management database (CMDB) is needed to hold such details.

Developing the functional design needs input from the users and business plans. The acceptance criteria derived from this input are expressed in general terms and will have to be translated to clear IT requirements. The resulting functional specification is approved by the project steering group.

The next step is to consider the organisational aspects of the IT solution. Both the operational management and the incorporation of operational management processes have to be defined. For example, it will have to be considered how incident management will support the new digital services, and how availability management will measure and monitor its availability. Additionally, responsibilities will have to be allocated and operating procedures will have to be written.

The technical design of the IT solution addresses issues – specific to various platforms – such as configurations and component sizes. The technical design shows how the IT solution will eventually be incorporated into the existing infrastructure.

The design phase should determine the working environments needed for each of the phases of the deployment project.

Build phase

During the build phase we advise having a development environment, which is isolated from the testing, acceptance and production environments, to prevent any premature impact on operational systems. If several disciplines are working on the IT solution during the build phase, we advise structuring their activities such that their development and testing activities are isolated. However, in some cases the new IT solution will have to use the existing production environment even as it is being developed. In that case, the best solution to facilitate this with the smallest possible impact will have to be selected. Improvement will play a critical part in this, as will an up-to-date CMDB and/or asset management capability.

During the build phase the documentation for the systems is written to prepare for their handover. Apart from the *technical* impact on the existing systems, the impact of the new systems on the IT infrastructure *capacity* will also have to be considered. This is often overlooked.

Review & Validation

Improvement

- Review all features of the product or service
- Validate whether they meet the requirements and constraints of the strategic objectives

 ... from a business service perspective

 ... from an information service perspective

 ... from an application service perspective

 ... from a technology service perspective

Review & Validation

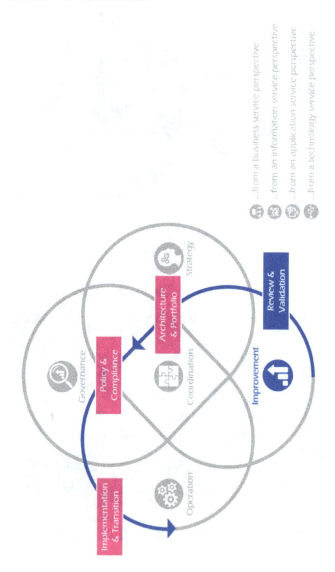

Figure 5.4: Review & Validation of touchstone elements

Review & Validation is the role that ensures all objectives have been covered, the requirements have been met and the solution has an acceptable functional fit with the four strands of enterprise DNA: business, information, applications/services and technology. Strategic activities regarding the architecture must be in line with policy; if not, the operational activities will not be contributing to the decisions made at board level. It is a key activity in enabling the enterprise to move forward in development of new services, because validation means that we can be certain the enterprise architecture will not be jeopardised.

Review & Validation (Figure 5.4) will examine the objectives regarding *Policy & Compliance* and *Effectiveness & Efficiency*, and as a natural extension will lay the foundation for the tasks of *Implementation & Transition.*

Architecture & Portfolio functions and *Policy & Compliance* contribute to the validation. The tasks undertaken should not be a surprise to anyone who has ever contributed to the development of an IT-driven service. Whether technology or software, or looking at data, it is important to test the functionality of anything that has been built. *Design & Realisation* might be the sexy job, but the mundane and often tedious task of testing is much more important because it might save a lot of money or embarrassment – or both. *Implementation & Transition* will (or should), of course, catch anything that was missed, but by then it may be too late to prevent expensive revisions. See also Appendix E.

Review & Validation

Programmes of change aimed at meeting performance targets will need to pay particular attention to the review phase and to the evaluation of programme outcomes. The enterprise will be concerned to establish that the target performance levels have been achieved, but some thought should also be given to establishing the role of the change programme in meeting the objectives.

In complex programmes of enterprise improvement, it can be difficult or even impossible to establish, after the event, that specific activities or policies in the change programme gave rise to identifiable and quantifiable improvements. Chains of cause and effect must be carefully considered in planning the change, and monitored during implementation. The approach to measurement of performance improvements and other objectives must be considered as part of the planning of the change programme, and not tacked on later as an afterthought. Things to think about:

- Be open minded about how requirements could be met (i.e. encouraging innovation where appropriate).
- Consider collaboration with others, e.g. partners (*Sourcing & Sponsoring*).
- Opt for evidence-based strategies where possible, i.e. learning lessons from what has worked for others – or didn't work.
- Ensure close engagement with stakeholders to ensure that their needs are accurately reflected in the requirements specification and end result.
- Be realistic about what can be delivered (enterprise capability and capacity to implement/absorb the change).
- Be clear about what the enterprise wants – do we understand what would/could meet the business need?
- Be clear when engaging with the market – do they understand what we want?
- Other than that, life is fairly straightforward and we can all get back on Twitter to distract ourselves.

Operation

Implementation
& Transaction

Deployment &
Maintenance

Contracts &
Agreements

Service &
Support

 ... from a business service perspective

 ... from an information service perspective

 ... from an application service perspective

 ... from a technology service perspective

CHAPTER SIX: THE CHALLENGE OF OPERATION

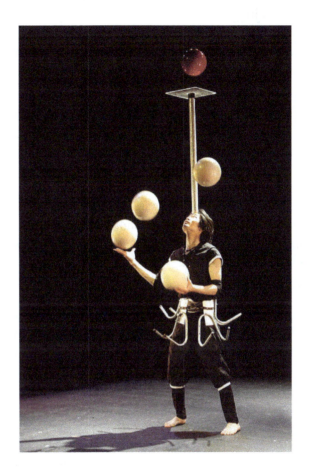

Keeping everything 'in the air'

The front line

We consider Operation as the ability of this unit of the enterprise to juggle many resources with the goal of keeping everything 'in the air'. In this chapter we will look at the role of Operation in more detail with regard to the big-picture IT4B model.

Good information service design, through *Design & Realisation*, will result in everything running smoothly and no one will care about contracts or service levels. Bad information service design will cause operational issues and incidents that must be addressed, and it is essential that monitoring activities have been designed and work well so that feedback can be provided. Governance policies, strategic decisions and design and/or build decisions, and *Sourcing & Sponsoring* all impact the business information processing in this domain.

Operation and IT

The operational processes within the IT enterprise concern not only the managed objects (the stuff that performs the magic, the digital services, the processing and the chunks of wire and metal and plastic) but also the interaction between them and their contribution to the delivery of IT services. Generating and assessing events (messages from monitoring systems) is an important aspect of operations. Too often, however, it becomes the focus rather than consideration of the efficiency and effectiveness of the digital services. Events are identified by operations all day and all night. Staff decide if they should be logged and processed as incidents and escalate them for attention where necessary. This barrage of resolving problems is just one activity among many that include the following example management processes:

- Managing business needs for IT.
- Managing infrastructure and digital service events.
- Operational control of digital services, components and configurations.
- Monitoring the workload, job scheduling, customer experience testing and resilience testing.
- Managing the storage capacity, backups and service recovery.
- Security management.
- Managing the operational support processes.
- Proactive operational management.

Output (and outcome)

The essential 'outcome' of Operation is *Deployment & Maintenance* of the new or improved digital services commissioned by the board. The process of ensuring this 'outcome' is, to a greater extent than in any other domain, present in the deployment of services or products that are outputs, i.e. Improvements, implemented RFCs and new technologies, that arose from *Need & Value*, and which were analysed in some form in *Developments & Trends*.

Necessary improvements will be (or at least should be) in line with the business mission and will almost certainly require a reassessment of the operational capabilities. The pivotal role of *Contracts & Agreements* in the centre of the Operation domain cannot be underestimated. Such instruments will be vital to establish a means of demonstrating compliance with policy directives.

The services resulting from developing new or improved digital services might well be subject to different forms of contractual agreements; operational performance measuring will be a key activity in demonstrating that business benefits have been achieved (or not). We have included Appendix F to expand on issues relating to Performance.

It might be that the digital services have been poorly designed (or implemented), or it might mean that improvements must be made to understanding data sources (whether from public sources such as the ubiquitous Internet, or from information chain partners or from customers).

In the gyroscope, the central element of Operation shown in Figure 6.1, *Contracts & Agreements*, is focused on enterprise business operations through a twin focus on *Service & Support* and *Implementation & Transition*. In turn, these activities contribute to the overall *Objectives & Requirements* of the enterprise by fulfilling the business mission because appropriate services have transitioned into use and are successfully deployed and maintained (*Deployment & Maintenance*). *Contracts & Agreements* outputs are a product of the activities initiated in the Governance domain. A direction will have been established that assessed *Sourcing & Sponsoring* options and architectural capabilities based on *Roles & Responsibilities*.

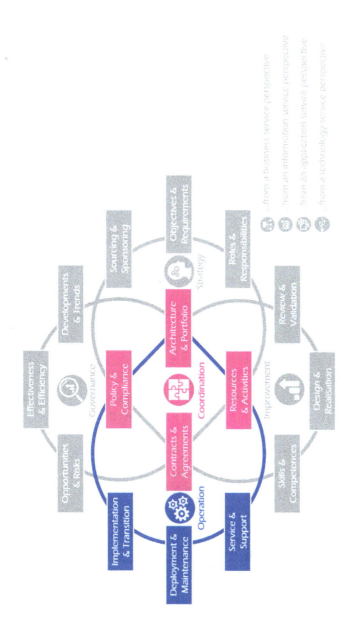

Figure 6.1: Touchstone elements and Operation

The Operation domain is often termed 'the daily processing domain' because it relates directly to functioning (or often non-functioning) data services. Digital information systems exist to support the business processes and to ensure that they proceed as efficiently and effectively as possible. It almost goes without saying that it is of considerable importance that services continue to work well and their effective use is guaranteed. This does not only concern the availability and the technical working of the application (subjects of IT infrastructure management and application management) but also functional working and application possibilities for the users.

In the Operation domain, in Figure 6.1, digital services that are consumed will be subject to either or both service agreements or contractual agreements. Operational services (digital or otherwise) are deployed as a result of changes or innovations designed to improve things for the enterprise.

Deployment & Maintenance is the function of deploying new and existing solutions and accepting output from the Improvement domain in general. The pivotal role of *Contracts & Agreements* in the centre of the Operation domain becomes clear when you consider that the services began their journey way back when *Design & Realisation* received approval to proceed with development. The designs proceeded through *Implementation & Transition* and *Service & Support*.

As we have mentioned elsewhere, you could start the journey of change/improvement from any point on the IT4B 'gyroscope'.

However, being at the sharp end of digital processing means using the digital information services available, processing new information, realising that what you have is not what you need, and in enterprises where the public at large is the customer, you also must deal with the pressure of providing good service. Here, again, four perspectives (business, service, information and technology) are inevitably linked because all four are linked to the customer experience.

Contracts & Agreements

Operation

- Identify the amount of resources and activities the product or service requires
- Identify the customers expectations of the product or service
- Ensure and maintain the customer relationship

 ... from a business service perspective

 ... from an information service perspective

 ... from an application service perspective

 ... from a technology service perspective

Contracts & Agreements

Managing contracts and service performance

Try enforcing a service level agreement and you will start to understand the difference between a contract and an agreement. A contract is legally enforceable, whereas an agreement can be ignored, broken or simply unsupported.

There are important differences between contracts (and agreements) for projects, although many of the principles are similar. Private finance (and IT outsourcing) contracts typically run for years; construction contracts are usually relatively short term, even if it takes a year or two to build something.

What is contract management?

Identifying how much a contract will cost to manage should be part of all discussions; the same is true of managing an SLA – what is this going to cost you to manage versus the benefit you expect to gain?

Contract management is the process that ensures both parties to a contract fully meet their respective obligations as efficiently and effectively as possible in order to deliver the business and operational objectives required from the contract and in particular to provide value for money. The UK government estimated that managing a contract typically requires resources for contract management that are equivalent to 2% of the contract value.

UK government guidance considers such due diligence an integral part of the 'intelligent (or informed) customer' capability.

Intelligent/informed customer capability

Intelligent customer capability combines in-depth knowledge of the department and its business and understanding of what the provider can and cannot do (*Sourcing & Sponsoring* in our model). It is vital that the individuals or teams responsible for managing services on the customer side have this kind of capability. The aim is to reduce misunderstanding between customer and provider and to avoid mistakes before they happen.

Intelligent customer *skills and competence* must also be retained for the whole life of the contract, so that the enterprise does not end up without enough understanding and knowledge of the services being provided to manage them effectively, or carry out an effective recompetition.

Among other things, the intelligent customer role helps the enterprise gain a common understanding between customer and service provider(s) of service expectations and possible achievement, uses service quality monitors as a basis for demonstrating ongoing value for money and service improvements, and ensures that benefits are achieved that recognise the full investment in business change; this is the element group *Effectiveness & Efficiency* and it is not solely applicable to the IT component of business services.

Managing multiple interfaces

In practice, you may have a wide range of customers with differing needs, both inside and outside the enterprise. In addition, your contractual arrangements could involve a number of providers in a complex supply chain and/or a prime contractor with responsibility for the selection and performance of subcontractors.

Where service provision arrangements are complex, the important areas for consideration include:

- Where risk lies and who will manage it; and
- The value chain: which services or service components add the most value, in that they make direct or critical contributions to realising objectives, perhaps in areas where the enterprise lacks capability – the services that justify a greater amount of proactive management.

Who is involved?

Contract managers representing both the customer and supplier/provider have a key role; there will also be input from the 'intelligent/informed customer', providing the interface between customers and providers. Ideally, the people involved in contract negotiation during the procurement process will take on a contract management role.

The same is true of SLAs; keep in mind that the SLA will almost certainly be discussed by well-meaning amateurs rather than by trained legal or procurement professionals. The popularity of IT-related SLAs is largely because IT people decided that users needed to be aware of their responsibilities; of course, IT also wanted users to be aware of IT responsibilities, but forgot that users do not particularly care about IT or about what IT people think.

Critical success factors

What are useful critical success factors? A contract is being managed successfully if the following conditions are met:

- The arrangements for service delivery continue to be satisfactory to both the customer and supplier/provider.

- Expected business benefits and value for money are being realised; requiring a focus on benefits management.
- The customer knows its obligations under the contract.
- Absence of dispute.
- No surprises (best of luck with that one).

Foundations for contract management

Throughout the procurement process, emphasis is likely to be on why the contract is being established and on whether the provider will be able to deliver in service and technical terms. If it is not, it is probably doomed from the start. It is essential to consider how the contract will work once it has been awarded. Professionals do this; SLA amateurs rarely do so.

Management of contracts, especially where there is a partnership, usually requires some flexibility on both sides and a willingness to adapt the terms of the contract (and/or SLA) to reflect a rapidly changing world. Problems are certain to surface that could not be foreseen when the contract was awarded; where SLAs are concerned, problems are almost guaranteed.

As the customer, you must have a clear business mission or vision and objectives, coupled with a clear understanding of how the contract will contribute to them. There must also be a clear understanding of the provider objectives, including the dirty business of making a profit. You must be able to recognise and get agreed at executive management level the need for the service provider to achieve their objectives, including making a reasonable margin, perhaps as part of a risk/reward arrangement.

Both sides need managers who can manage board-level individuals to make decisions for the benefit of the joint relationship (you can be certain that this will be a challenge when some issues are examined in isolation). There must be people with the right interpersonal and management skills to manage these relationships on a peer-to-peer basis and at multiple levels in the enterprise.

Other issues

Other areas that need to be considered in depth before the contract is signed include:

- What is the likelihood of the provider team changing after award of contract, leading to a lack of continuity?
- If the provider is a consortium, it is essential to understand how the consortium members handle things to ensure that problems are resolved quickly and constructively. It might be necessary to ensure that all members of the consortium share the same quality management system and/or escalation procedures.
- Can you ensure that enough time is allowed for the provider's learning curve in understanding the complexity of your business? What does the provider know about your business and current IT operation and how will they bridge any shortfalls in knowledge or capability?
- What level of control is needed and what are the processes for managing the contract that will give you the level of control you need?
- You must be able to understand the answers to complex technical issues and enter into dialogue with the provider, meaning that an intelligent/informed customer capability must be retained with sufficient expertise to

understand the technical direction in which the provider is taking your enterprise.

- Consider how the provider can ensure that they always provide you sufficient skilled resources, and evaluate the risk that other customers' accounts might take priority.
- Evaluate the quality of the provider team. Evaluate if they have sufficient standing within their enterprise to ensure that they will be able to deliver the resources you require.
- Where SLAs are involved, are you certain that you know enough about IT to judge the service criteria set out? Appendix F discusses Performance.

Implementation & Transition

Operation

- Ensure a seamless commissioning of new developments
- Establish a programme for ensuring continuity of normal operations during the transition

 ... from a business service perspective
 ... from an information service perspective
 ... from an application service perspective
 ... from a technology service perspective

Implementation & Transition

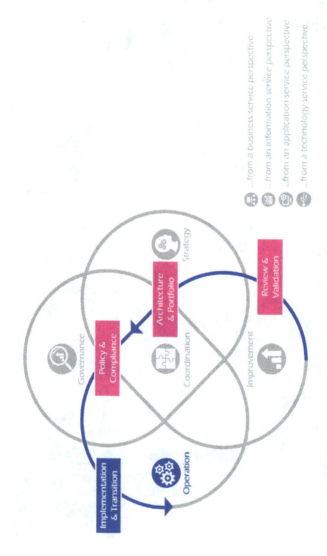

Figure 6.2: Implementation & Transition ensures compliance with goals

Figure 6.2 illustrates the key role of *Implementation & Transition,* which is needed to take forward the developments made in the Improvement domain. As mentioned earlier, goal setting at board level is one thing, but ensuring that Operation can deliver as required is another.

The dependencies between *Policy & Compliance* (ensuring the enterprise policies, benefits and outcomes will be as directed), *Review & Validation* (ensuring the services are robust, secure and constructed with strategic intent), and *Architecture & Portfolio* (compliance with architectural and portfolio management principles embraced by the enterprise) are highlighted.

As with all of the discussions about the IT4B model, you need to keep in mind that these highlighted dependencies do not preclude others; the model is intended to illustrate that dependencies are everywhere, and that at certain times in development some dependencies have more impact than others.

Anyway, implement what? Well, the best way to discuss I*mplementation & Transition* is to select an example and walk through it. Consider how to implement business continuity management, which seems a reasonably important activity.

You could use a four-stage lifecycle for business continuity management:

- Stage 1: Initiation (a strategy level activity):
  - o Set the policy and scope for business continuity management (*Policy & Compliance*).
  - o Establish a business continuity management initiative and a sense of urgency (see John Kotter).
- Stage 2: Requirements and strategy objectives:

- o Assesses potential business impacts, opportunities and risks (*Opportunities & Risk*).
- o Identify and evaluate options (*Review & Validation*).
- o Develop a cost-effective strategy. This strategy must balance business priorities against the risks of failing to provide functionality, and matched with costs of adopting particular business continuity options.
- Stage 3: Implementation:
  - o Establish a programme for achieving business continuity.
  - o Implement the business continuity management strategy.
  - o Undertake initial testing of the business continuity plan *(Deployment & Maintenance)*.
- Stage 4: Operational management/recovery:
  - o Maintains the strategy, plans and procedures (*Service & Support*). During this stage you need to look at education and awareness, review of the plans and risks (with their associated reduction measures), testing of the plans, and controlling changes to the strategy and the plans so these are maintained to be consistent with each other
  - o Training people to produce the strategy and plans as well as to undertake the actions embodied within the plans (*Skills & Competence*).

There is an overall need to assure the quality and applicability of the plans (*Effectiveness & Efficiency*). In this context, 'quality' refers to adaptability, completeness, data quality, efficiency, friendliness/usability (very important as the plan will only be used in a time of chaos or disaster), maintainability, portability, reliability, resilience, security, testability and timeliness.

Recovery of normal operations needs to be the final – and planned for – objective of business continuity management.

The concepts and procedures would be broadly similar for any activity or service that needs to be transitioned into Operation.

So, the essence of *Implementation & Transition* is its role to ensure a seamless implementation of new developments, mindful of each of the perspectives: business, information, applications/services and technology.

Deployment & Maintenance

Operation

- Ensure that the product or service is being delivered as agreed, to the required level of performance and quality
- Ensure the continuity of operations, keeping unplanned interruptions to a minimum
- Plan for optimisation of future continuity

 ... from a business service perspective

 ... from an information service perspective

 ... from an application service perspective

 ... from a technology service perspective

Deployment & Maintenance

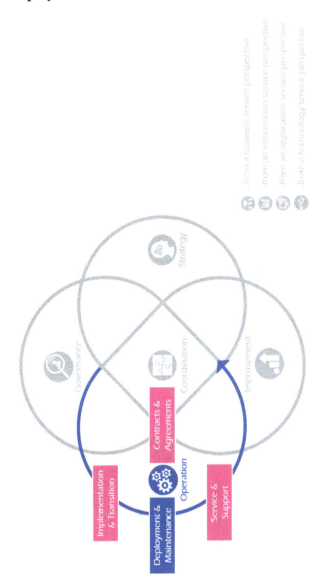

Figure 6.3: Deployment & Maintenance of improved services

Effective delivery requires that interdependencies are managed effectively. Interdependencies can occur anywhere: between programmes, projects or individual deliverables. They are often complex and dynamic, so need to be assessed and managed as an ongoing process. Deployment of the resources needed to realise design objectives is different to delivery of a programme or project. Until (or unless) the new or improved services are in use, and are effective in operation, delivery is incomplete irrespective of who signed off the work in the delivery processes.

In this domain, it is essential to understand the contracts and agreements that underpin the delivered improvements to services and what is needed at the front line to support the use of the services. In the earlier discussion about implementation, we made clear that *Implementation & Transition* is concerned primarily with ensuring that goal setting and operation are in balance. Goal setting should also have covered the issues of *Service & Support* implementation and the need to comply with contractual agreements.

Scope of work

Deployment and maintenance issues should be clear at the stage of scoping the work. While defining the scope of the work, you will need to judge:

- Who should steer, independently quality review, or produce the deliverables;
- Whether the risks, dependencies and constraints have been recognised and understood at all levels;
- Whether your plans are well enough developed to allow you to anticipate risk, and manage it with countermeasures and contingency plans;

- How to sustain your focus on producing and implementing suitable deliverables to achieve the intended outcomes;
- Whether this is a programme, made up of a number of interrelated projects, or a discrete project.
- How many separate work strands or streams are needed and how these should be aligned to deliver objectives;
- What mix of skills, numbers of people, money and time each strand, and the programme/project overall, will demand; and
- How you will know that you are succeeding or adjust your plans if you are not – including cancelling the project or programme with minimum time and resources wasted if you are no longer sufficiently confident of delivering.

These high-level indicators of delivery preface the activities that will take place as part of an application services delivery lifecycle (Agile led or 'traditionally' developed), and ultimately to delivery of digital services.

Checklist/activities

Any digital service being designed will have cycled through some form of development lifecycle, whether Agile in name or Agile in process, or managed using an established project management method. Any sensible application management lifecycle emphasises the links between application development and service management and the activities in each phase of the lifecycle to maintain these aspects. The activities are usually performed as phases under the control of a project or a release.

Requirements

In this phase, the requirements of a new or modified application are defined on the basis of the needs of the business. The application requirements are closely related to the primary business drivers of the business process to be supported by the application. In other words, if you started being Agile with IT, think again; you need to know what the SRO has commissioned for the business and business objectives that digital services will either support, improve or enable. The following requirement types can be distinguished:

- Functional requirements describe the behaviour of an application and can be expressed in terms of services, activities, tasks or functions. Functional requirements can be defined using context diagrams or use cases, and IT has a wealth of choices open for ways to document those. The use cases would be most useful to describe the functional aspects of an SLA, and as a basis for functional acceptance tests.

- Usability requirements should be described that ensure the application meets the user expectations regarding ease of use. Together with the non-functional requirements, the user requirements can be used to define an application's quality attributes.

- Non-functional requirements determine an application's limitations in terms of volumes, capacity, performance, manageability, operability, support and security. These requirements primarily relate to service management. The non-functional requirements should be used to define an application's quality attributes, which then provides the basis for the production acceptance tests.

It is important to test the various requirements. This is often difficult as there may not be a specific method to test abstract requirements. There may be a considerable number of requirements, and some may conflict. The feasibility of the requirements can be determined through prototyping, metaplan sessions, peer reviews and presentations.

Design

In the design phase, the requirements provided by the business and the IT enterprise are translated into application characteristics. Whether 'Agile' or not, the design phase should deliver not just one but several possible designs. In general terms, the following designs are used:

- The architectural guidelines used by an enterprise for application design and the operational models.
- The application's functional design.
- The operational model of the environment in which the application runs, such as the infrastructure and the systems management environment.

During the design phase the programme/project manager will have to take a number of decisions to balance the available resources, the project plan and the functionality to be provided. This balance is not always obtained in projects, which results in the non-functional requirements being abandoned. It is surprising how sacrifices are made when it comes down to staying within budget, and stupid decisions are often made because they are easy to make, not because they are the right decisions. Similarly, stupid decisions are made when delivery on time becomes tricky. Resources, plans and functionality – always a compromise, eh? However, this triangle of resources can be defined with some accuracy once a number of working products have been delivered:

The key business drivers

- The project objectives and scope.
- The functional requirements.
- The non-functional requirements.
- The application designs.
- The project plans.

Build

In the building phase the digital service application and operational model are prepared for deployment. Application components are coded or purchased, integrated and tested. To ensure that the management of future iterations of the application management lifecycle is considered when an application is built, the development team should aim to meet both the functional and non-functional requirements. And don't listen to anyone who tells you Agile methods can avoid this step.

Consistent programming guidelines

The primary reason for applying consistent programming guidelines is that it will be easier for everyone to read, understand and manage the application. Every enterprise should at least have a generic set of guidelines, which facilitates application maintenance and provides the developers with enough flexibility to implement the application's logic and functionality. These programming guidelines not only make the applications easier to maintain but also provide better opportunities for using tools to manage the applications. However, enterprises should ensure that the guidelines do not become too complex or extensive.

In that case the creativity of the developer would be focused on the application of the guidelines rather than meeting the functional and non-functional requirements.

Application-independent guidelines

Several application-independent guidelines may be defined to assist the maintenance and management of an information system and its applications:

- Application frameworks – architectures, which identify which module or object is used for certain functions and tasks of the application. An application framework makes it possible for generic tasks (which are not directly related to the business process) to be handled by a single module or object. The advantage of these frameworks is that the cost of building the information systems is greatly reduced, while making maintenance significantly easier.

- Templates and code generation – many development tools use templates to build applications. Developers can use these tools to modify templates to meet the design requirements. Other tools not only offer templates but can also generate large sections of code further to detailed application designs. The advantage of using these tools is that they enforce standardisation.

- Built-in tools – there should be uniformity in controlling drivers and software for generic functions such as databases and communications protocols. Applications should also provide APIs for interfacing to system management tools. There are several guidelines for incorporating such interfaces in applications.

Application testing

Testing is not simply an activity carried out after building an application; it serves as an integrated quality management instrument throughout the full application management lifecycle. The test activities in the earlier phases mostly included assessments such as peer reviews and walk-throughs. When the software is built, both assessments and actual tests can be carried out.

In all phases, testing needs to be performed on the application's functionality and its non-functional aspects (non-functional aspects testing is known as 'operability testing'). The most important testing should, of course, be that of the customer experience. If the customer is not happy, every form of testing, from code to resilience, is largely wasted. Where significant change to the business processes has been made (and if a digital-first strategy has been employed, change will be significant), training will be needed before the customer can properly assess the usefulness of the new IT services.

As applications normally progress several times through the application management lifecycle, they will be tested on several occasions. Consequently, test environment management is an important, but often neglected, element of application management.

Deploy

Deployment ensures that the IT solutions can be incorporated into the enterprise in accordance with the planning process guidelines. To ensure that all activities can be monitored, deployment should be implemented as a project, in cooperation with Improvement personnel. The process should ensure that all stakeholders approve the plans, after which the solution is designed and then implemented.

This process is normally implemented as a single project or in a number of consecutive stages or sub-projects. Each deployment is essentially a change programme or change project (compared with change management). It starts with developing the project plans and ends with the implemented IT solutions.

Deployment projects progress through five stages:

1. Initiation – defining the project objectives and business case, identifying risks, selecting stakeholders to sit on the steering group.
2. Planning – development of the plans into a project structure, division into deliverables, detailing of the deliverables, budgeting, and determining the cycle times.
3. Execution – design, build, testing, deployment, and handover of the technical and organisational components.
4. Completion – evaluation of the project and discharge of the project team.

The execution stage progresses through the following phases:

- Design
- Build
- Acceptance test
- Rollout

Handover

In the deployment phase the application and the accompanying operational model are introduced into the production environment. The operational model is incorporated into the existing production environment, and the application is installed in the new environment, using standard installation procedures.

The deployment phase involves the following activities:

- Planning the deployment
- Organising the deployment team
- Approving the deployment
- Distributing applications
- Pilot roll-outs

A well-planned deployment will not only reduce the service interruptions but also significantly reduce the cost of providing the services. The following issues should be considered when planning the deployment:

QUESTIONS

ISSUES

What should be deployed?

- Is it clear what the application to be deployed will do, what it will consist of, and in what environment it will be deployed? What are the key business drivers covered by the application? Are there critical business requirements covered by the application?
- Who are the users?
- What users or user communications will be affected by the deployment?
- Will these users need special training?
- Where are the users based?
- Are the users based in the same building as the infrastructure that the application runs on? If not, how will this affect logistics?

- When should the deployment be completed?
- Should the application be completed by a particular date or is the deployment date flexible?
- Why is the change being deployed?
- Does the change relate to an identified problem or are new functions deployed?
- Do the users understand why the change is deployed?
- What is essential to a successful deployment?
- When will the deployment be successful? What are the criteria for a completed deployment?

Questions surrounding deployment

A number of checklists and documents should be completed and approved before the deployment is allowed to start. These include:

- Deployment management checklist
- Deployment plan and schedule
- Back-out document
- Sign-off document

Approval involves the change management process using one or a number of RFCs with CAB approving the deployment of the application.

Deployment planning and back-out involves the release management process.

Operate

A Gartner study indicated that 40% of service interruptions are due to operator errors and 40% to application bugs. It is therefore important that the application should largely run unattended once in production. This means that automatic start-up and shutdown scripts, reporting and recovery facilities are needed. When the operational status of an application is recovered it is important to be aware of its operational status and what components are affected. Each application includes a number of components:

- The application itself
- Server-specific configuration details
- Log files
- System files
- User-specific configuration details
- User details
- Network connections

The impact of any service interruptions is minimised through effective design of the applications and the infrastructure and through a number of preventative maintenance activities taken by the operational team. These activities should be planned and documented with tools, resources and training provided as part of the application project. Maintenance is discussed in more detail in Appendix G.

Service & Support

Operation

- Ensure that the product or service is being used as agreed, to the required level of performance and quality
- Ensure an optimal communication with customers with regard to feedback and change requests

 ... from a business service perspective

 ... from an information service perspective

 ... from an application service perspective

 ... from a technology service perspective

Service & Support

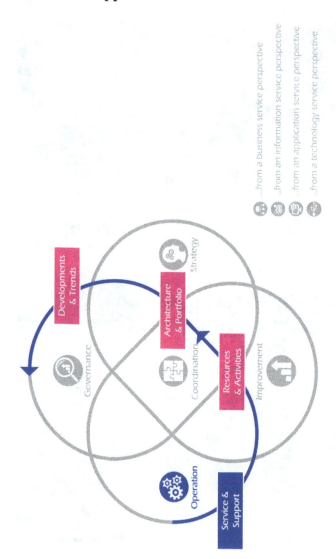

Figure 6.4: The Service & Support feedback loop

Figure 6.4 illustrates how *Service & Support* processes provide essential feedback about how new or improved services have been delivered and deployed, and received (by that we mean both in terms of acceptance and satisfaction), and how operational resources have been impacted. The feedback should also inform management about how well the strategy for improvement performed.

Where the strategy was sound, everything identified in the architectural and portfolio planning should be in line with both the *Developments & Trends* identified at board level and with the resources brought to bear to ensure improvements would be successful. Where the strategy was unsound, you can be certain that problems will have arisen that will make that clear.

More often than not, Operation finds itself on the receiving end of developments. In many cases they have had just a minor influence on the improvements needed to a service. It is not uncommon that during the *Implementation & Transition* process the project encounters resistance from the end users, making *foie gras*-like change management practices inevitable to force-feed the 'innovation' to the enterprise.

Could this be the root cause of the widespread belief that people have an intrinsic reluctance to change? A quick analysis of our history proves otherwise. The adaptation of change is almost what defines us as human beings. We simply love to adopt new technologies and include them in our day-to-day lives. That was true in the 15th century, as we saw in the introduction to this book about the art of painting. And it is still true today where technology even defines the way we communicate and maintain our relationships.

Of course, there can be resistance to change within our enterprises. Often it arises from uninformed sources. But let's leave the 'business dark ages' behind and enter into a renaissance of digital transformation of our enterprises.

So how is it that, contrary to our personal lives, we have difficulty adapting to change within our enterprises? Can it be our top-down approach to change? Nothing wrong with that, but there has to be a balance. Anyway, how many revolutions do you know that started top-down?

For this reason, we began this part of the discussion with one possible navigation of the IT4B operating model – beginning bottom-up. *Service & Support* can be the starting point for Improvement or innovation. The 'operators' are in possession of customer feedback and user incidents. This is where business perception meets customer and user reality. The perfect place to spot opportunities for improvement! How?

- Analysis of customer and user feedback and incidents can be a valuable input for improvement.
- Viability check by *Resources & Activities* to show initial estimates of the effort to obtain successful improvement.
- Viability check by *Architecture & Portfolio* to show initial estimates of impact on existing components and ongoing projects.
- *Developments & Trends* providing initial solution scenarios.

The idea is to minimise effort and impact and maximise the results. As with all of the elements we have described, navigation can begin (or end) wherever it is appropriate for your enterprise.

Service & Support **for the business**

The perspective we adopt in this book is that the business manager identifies and articulates the business needs that the (IT) service should meet. In the ITIL world this is often misunderstood because 'business' is assumed to be IT. Information (applications) is used by the business, the infrastructure is an essential evil, and it can be outsourced if the IT services are not available as specified in the business service design or if data is corrupted.

Users of the service provided should give feedback on how the service and the relationship is going with IT services, and may also request changes to the service.

In IT4B, Operation activities (frameworks such as ITIL group these under 'service management') fall into three main areas:

1. *Deployment & Maintenance* of services (service delivery in ITIL) ensures that the service is being delivered as agreed, to the required level of performance and quality.
2. *Roles & Responsibilities* (which can be termed 'relationship management') keeps the relationship between the business and IT open and constructive, resolving tensions and identifying problems early on.
3. *Contracts & Agreements* handles the formal governance of the contract and changes to the contract documentation.

Where services were outsourced either in part or wholly, what is often known as *'Intelligent customer capabilities'* should be in place to provide an expert interface between the enterprise and its providers *(Skills & Competences).*

Service & Support tasks will be carried out by a combination of roles: service manager, contract manager and relationship manager. However, depending on the size and complexity of the arrangement, it is possible that two or more roles may be filled by the same individual, or covered by the same team. There will also be a contract manager on the provider's side.

All four perspectives – Business, Data/Information, Applications (services) and Technology – will impact service operations and feedback should be elicited for each. The feedback will influence future planning for improvement of various aspects of service and support and can directly influence the enterprise's technology transformation agenda.

Any improvements identified in Operation will directly influence two 'touchstone' element pairs: *Resources & Activities* and *Architecture & Portfolio*. Operation may be always on the receiving end of developments, but that does not mean they have no influence over change. In many cases Operation is the instrument of change because they are on the receiving end when things go awry.

Supporting the user of digital services

Business managers should aim to provide optimum quality digital information and data services, cognisant of the resources available. Quality is determined by fitness for purpose, and quality digital information and data services are those that consistently meet business needs and customer requirements. *Contracts & Agreements* is the key touchstone element. Effective liaison between service suppliers and their customers is an essential aspect of supply of quality information and data services. Information service suppliers must understand the purposes to which the services are put, and provide services that fulfil these purposes.

Users of digital information and data services are the customers of the (IT) services supplier. Whether or not they are being charged for services, they should be treated as customers, and their views taken into account. Suppliers must continually seek to improve their standard of service to customers. They must research and respond to customer views and effectively and efficiently support their use of services.

Once the new or changed services are available, *Implementation & Transition* activities, and all the supporting IT4B elements (assessments or perhaps training, manuals and so on) have been completed, Operation takes over the responsibilities for monitoring effectiveness and identifying any issues. Support for the services (*Service & Support*) should be provided centrally and locally where possible. Security measures, the perceived quality and the operational issues regarding the availability of the services and the problems associated with data being processed and retrieved will be the most likely cause of issues arising.

Identifying improvement to the digital business services should be uppermost in thinking and is part of the *Service & Support* activities. Even services that work effectively can be improved and a forum to raise improvement issues should be available, at least online.

Operational control of services, components and configurations

This process includes all activities related to component management, such as replacing, fixing and upgrading components. A number of these activities should use the change management processes, in particular as standard changes with approved work procedures and instructions, to ensure they are performed in a controlled manner and the results are visible through the CMDB. The main activities are:

- Installation – including defining acceptance criteria;
- De-installation – e.g. phasing out components;
- Distribution – of managed objects, e.g. through uploading and downloading;
- Operational management – including initialisation and configuration;
- Development and management of management tools – including integration with IT service management tools;
- Configuration and reconfiguration – resetting and modifying managed objects;
- Housekeeping and preventive maintenance – all routine processes for ensuring a resilient infrastructure, including:
  - Deleting log files;
  - Deleting temporary files;
  - Cleaning operational equipment and environments;
  - Maintaining and supporting systems and tools;
  - User and file authorisation and password management;
  - Preventive maintenance;
  - Shift handover and reporting; and
  - Operational reporting.
- Inventory and asset management – including identification, registration and verification of operational MOs and collecting information about changes to MO configurations. This primarily concerns collecting information about the present infrastructure

(e.g. using discovery tools), which can be used to verify and update the CMDB;

- Workload monitoring, job scheduling and resilience testing. This process includes creating and maintaining all operational plans related to infrastructure workloads:
  o Workload planning, job scheduling, controlling progress and resolving conflicts and failures.
  o Output and print schedule management.
  o Distribution and management of data and media, including file transmissions, backup media and physical document.
  o Resilience and failover arrangement testing, including standby, alternate site operation, business continuity and disaster recovery plans.
- Storage, backups and service recovery management. This process covers all aspects of information storage and data restores, such as:
  o Storage management and storage allocation;
  o System backups and restores;
  o Information management (what is stored, on what media and where); and
  o Database management and administration.

Keep in mind that there are many methods and frameworks focused on service management, principally ITIL, ETOM, MoF and lately IT4IT. All contain very useful advice, though none focus on information (data) as these frameworks arise from the infrastructure perspective. BiSL Next is the framework focused on the information/data needs. Adapt such guidance where it applies but beware of thinking data can be managed in the same way as hardware and networks.

Management of infrastructure events

In many enterprises, thanks to the excessive publicity focused on service management (that despite claims to the contrary, is *not* focused on information or information services), this is the main process in Operation, with all other operational processes arranged around it. The activities include:

- Event monitoring – monitoring trends and abnormal situations affecting the infrastructure and service managed objects;
- Event detection – observing alarms from managed objects;
- Event logging – collecting and storing information about managed object status transitions;
- Event assessment and filtering – analysis, possibly followed by choosing a resolution option;
- Event handling – identifying correlations between events, analysis and creating incidents;
- Event resolution – rectifying the abnormality and restoring services;
- Event closure – clearing events and closing incidents;
- Event lifecycle management – creating and improving the resolution process;
- Event classification – classifying and collating events consistent with incident and problem-handling procedures; and
- Event reporting – logging, reporting and analysing events.

Service & Support is a massive undertaking. Without it, however, digital information services cannot be effectively deployed and maintained.

CHAPTER SEVEN: DIGITAL READINESS AND INNOVATION

IT4B has been described throughout as a camera obscura for digital transformation. 'Who by?' you might ask. The answer is, of course, by us. As we have mentioned, David Hockney is one of a growing number of intellectuals and artists convinced that a camera obscura was used to project images that long-dead artists used as a means to paint almost photographic likenesses of models and locations (Figure 7.1). The minor detail that the model/location was upside down was solved by rotating the canvas.

IT4B carries that idea forward: project an image of the enterprise that is recognisable, but instead of applying paint, we apply well-researched and documented best practices to 'the image' to identify gaps in knowledge, skills, execution and, yes, technology. IT4B is not reinventing your favourite method, it is putting it into the context of improvement and identifying any potential gaps.

Figure 7.1: Turning the world upside down

The IT4B model is sufficiently generic to pull together the process elements common to most, if not all, enterprises. The IT4B profiles are created to focus on capabilities (elements in the IT4B model) and on the enterprise's overall readiness with regard to achievable benefits and possible innovations. The profiles can be generated in any order and in this example we start with Figure 7.2, using the canvas to project the good, bad or ugly picture of how well your enterprise operates or uses common processes. As we have described, it does so from four perspectives to ensure the projected model is as complete a picture as possible.

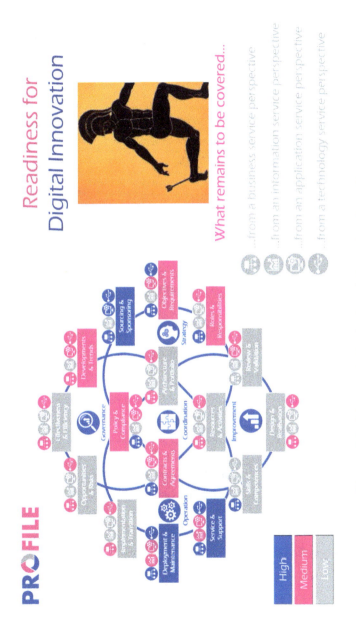

Figure 7.2: The good, the bad and the ugly of readiness

This profile model is used to provide insight into how to improve on the fit of your products and services to the needs of your target audience. The output shows where improvement is needed. We intend that when using IT4B your enterprise obtains a:

- Comprehensive improvement overview with regard to all your business processes, information flows, applications and technology;
- Translation of your business ambitions into an executable IT strategy;
- Collaboration structure for the business and IT domains where all roles and responsibilities are assigned within the existing organisation and (current) service providers;
- Complete set of competence profiles that will serve as a baseline for either customised training or recruitment; and
- Practical transformation *focus* that directs your enterprise in reaching its full potential.

The next step in this example is the Profile, which is shown in Figure 7.3.

The profile output here is designed to illustrate strengths and weaknesses that exist in the enterprise. Weaknesses must be addressed, otherwise it is clear that readiness is in question. The outputs will cover Benefits, Innovation and Operating model requirements, ensuring the essential link between goal setting and operation can be achieved.

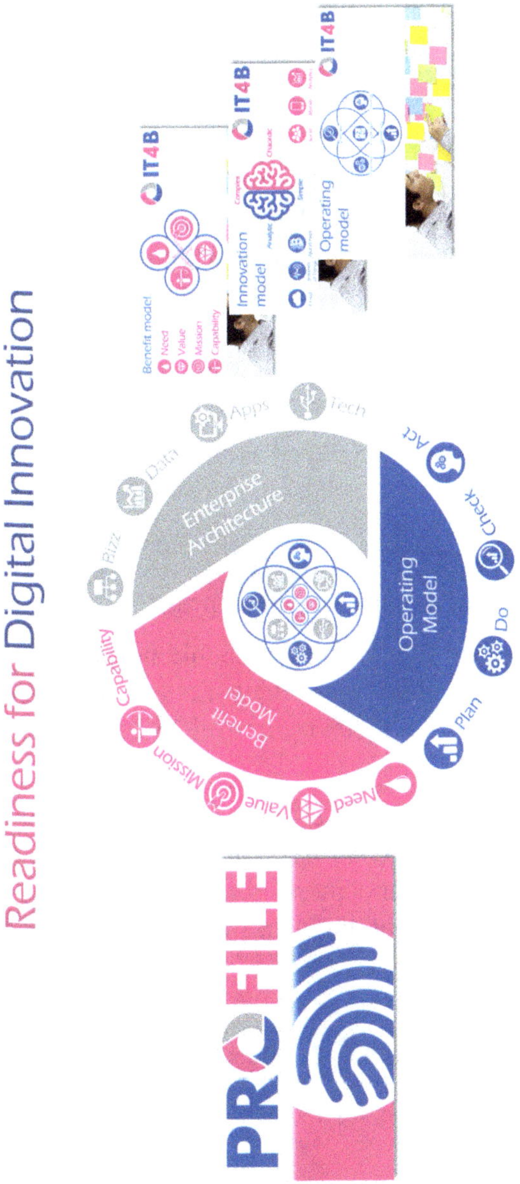

Figure 7.3: The enterprise digital profile

Now you might say that myriad frameworks, methods and models make this. Implement ITIL or TOGAF or IT4IT or PRINCE2® or whatever and the business will come running to your door begging IT to help. They won't.

No one framework can be used to transform business and IT, and IT4B is not intended to do that either; the most important uses of the model are to discover what capabilities exist in your enterprise (including capabilities in any or all of the above-mentioned frameworks and many others) *and* identify shortcomings and improvements in using them.

To illustrate how this works, we have selected two IT 'best practices' that are often employed as the means to transform or improve. COBIT is chosen because so many IT professionals think it is a business framework for improvement. The clue is in the 'IT' part of the acronym; COB*IT* isn't of any interest to the business.

That does not mean it is useless or should not be used; it is just a recognition that where frameworks and models exist, adherents will promote 'their' framework as being definitive and transformative.

COBIT (as with other well-documented models and frameworks) is excellent and has many uses. Though as we will explore, by using our camera obscura (Figure 7.4), it has certain limitations that can be identified using IT4B.

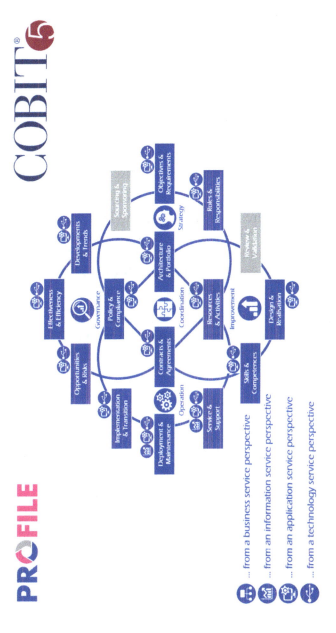

Figure 7.4: The limitations of using only COBIT

We also selected COBIT because it is actually fairly comprehensive, but two very important components are lacking: examining *Sourcing & Sponsoring* and ensuring proper *Review & Validation* of improvements.

If you don't think these components are important, you can ignore IT4B and move on. However, keep in mind that COBIT might be considered an audit framework but it is an IT audit framework and does not address either the business perspective or the information perspective with any degree of penetration.

We can further address the issue by using DevOps. DevOps is a movement; a cultural phenomenon that has eaten the lunch of process-dependent frameworks, and soundly spanked anything that takes any length of time to use or instantiate. But the business side still does not care.

Surprisingly, DevOps has more 'grey areas' than COBIT when viewed through our camera obscura (Figure 7.5).

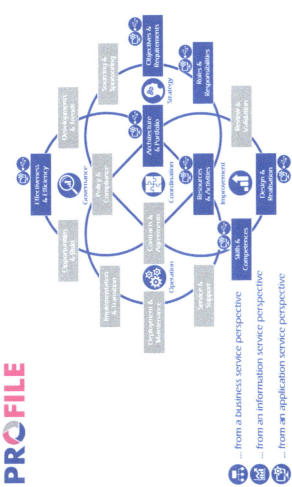

Figure 7.5: DevOps through the looking glass

... from a business service perspective

... from an information service perspective

... from an application service perspective

... from a technology service perspective

What is useful in DevOps is very, very useful, but just don't think it can be used for everything you need to do to transform your enterprise into digital superstardom.

What should be obvious from just these two examples is that nothing exists in the market that does everything you might need when it comes to applying best practices, and nothing exists that 'implements digital transformation', or 'business and IT integration', or any other claim to universal nirvana.

IT4B is the same. It does not 'implement' anything, it is a means to an end. IT4B provides the lens through which you view the needs of your enterprise, the problem areas, the organisational components that need to improve and how to use the many best practices in a coherent application to achieve transformation. Transformation is not instantaneous and it will require many resources, not least money.

IT4B will help you to join up all the dots in your enterprise to focus effort on improvement and innovation. As shown in Figure 7.6, it does act as the camera obscura.

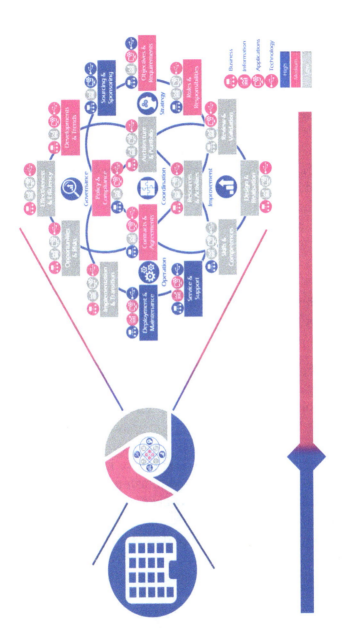

Figure 7.6: Camera obscura, focus, focus, focus

The digital profile you create (well, the one we recommended that you create) requires that you always consider four perspectives when contemplating digital transformation.

We also recommend that someone from the business side (not the 'business side of IT', a common error perpetrated by failing to recognise that many IT best practices do not improve *business* services because they focus on improving IT procedures) leads the improvement as the SRO. Not because they are necessarily more intelligent or innovative, but because digital transformation is focused on business and IT is the enabler, not the goal. It is generally much easier for a business SRO to understand the broad strokes of IT and how IT can be used than it is for an IT director to understand the subtleties of business.

Figure 7.5 illustrates our use of IT4B as the lens. The lens directs you to consider:

- The business perspective first: what are the goals of the enterprise, and do we understand the role IT could play? Are our IT-enabled business services doing what we need? Does our IT organisation know what we do, what we need and how to help?
- The information perspective: do we have access to the data we will need to enable transformation, and do we even know what data we need and where it can be found? How is our data secured, retrieved and used? Who is responsible for data definitions and usage?
- The services perspective: who is responsible for service design? Has the business/IT relationship been productive in the past? What is the business view of service provision and management and what is the IT view of how services are designed and supported?

- The technology perspective: does the business know how IT can be used to transform business and working practices? Does IT know how to explain to the business in comprehensible language the potential for IT in business? How reliant is the business on technology?

The perspectives are necessary to gather a comprehensive understanding of need and value; they also assist in gathering information about the future of the enterprise, the mission and the capabilities of the enterprise now and in the future.

Without this comprehensive understanding, it is not possible to create a roadmap for improvement.

In the next chapter we will introduce the outline of a case study that we have created to assist with understanding and using IT4B. You can use the outline in Chapter nine to think about the 'how to' elements of this chapter, or of course if you prefer, think of an internal project that fits the bill. Learning arises in many different ways; some people like to focus on something they know about when considering how to apply unfamiliar concepts, whereas some prefer to think about new ideas in a more abstract manner.

CHAPTER EIGHT: MYTHICAL AIRLINES CASE STUDY

Mythical Airlines Ltd

Readers familiar with Mythical Airlines will recall we used it as an example of the need to get business information requirements clear (when writing the BiSL Next guidance and guidance about collaborative business service design). Why? Well, everyone knows what an airline does (or should do), and everyone knows how badly they perform in so many areas relating to customers and because given the chance, we could all design a better airline. So here is your chance.

Imagine you have to travel from Schiphol, through London to New York. You make reservations via the Mythical portal, you check in the day before you go to Schiphol using the same portal and print a boarding pass. At Schiphol you use your boarding pass at the automatic check-in gates. After that you throw your luggage at the counter, navigate security, do some shopping at the duty free and finally board the aeroplane.

After about eight hours you arrive at JFK, get out, suffer the usual abuse from immigration, collect your luggage and finally exit through customs. Perhaps you have hired a car using Mythical because it has partners in the business, and you collect it from the car park, program the destination in the SatNav and drive to your hotel (also a Mythical partner).

Holiday or business or both, this sort of experience is common and when Mythical Airlines does what is expected, nobody has any idea what is hidden behind the scenes.

If you are responsible for organising the backstage services, however, you are aware that all the services that make up the experience are built on IT-driven processes. Without IT your experience would be a lot different and certainly not as smooth as described above. Until all the check-in terminals are down because of a massive IT failure, that is.

The IT interaction

All IT-intensive services that are being developed in an enterprise must contribute in one way or another, either as a primary activity, as part of the core or as part of a necessary secondary process to the enterprise business goals. In the past few years the distinction between primary and secondary processes has become more diffuse as execution of work and supporting processes becomes more difficult to separate. And airlines are no different.

It therefore does not come as a surprise that service developments or service changes vigorously attracts the attention of stakeholders within an enterprise. Business stakeholders want to be involved in the development and implementation or adaptation of highly IT-driven business services to ensure that different perspectives, interests and principles are included.

The first question in designing and building Mythical is: who are your stakeholders? The second is: do they want this airline to be Emirates or Ryanair? Are they filling a niche or innovating with an Uber approach to air travel?

What do they value: satisfied customers or money? The mission/capability/need/value conundrum is the starting point.

Think about service characteristics

Each of the four perspectives of business, information, applications/services and technology must be applied to designing airline services because of the dependencies.

It is imperative to understand the characteristics of IT-driven services and service offerings, understand service requirements and describe a structured approach to gather the right requirements for effective service solutions. After all, your life might depend on IT software running as it should in any airline. Now define the service. Depending on your perspective, it could be taking people from point A to point B. Another person might add the word 'safely'. Someone else might point out that buying a ticket is part of the service. What about onboard catering? And we have not even started to discuss the services that begin at the airport, such as check-in, baggage, or membership of frequent flyer clubs.

Figure 8.1 illustrates a very simplified example of what is (most of) the overall service of Mythical Airlines. The enterprise (that is, the owner of the airline) is in it, however, to make money, not *necessarily* to provide the best services to passengers.

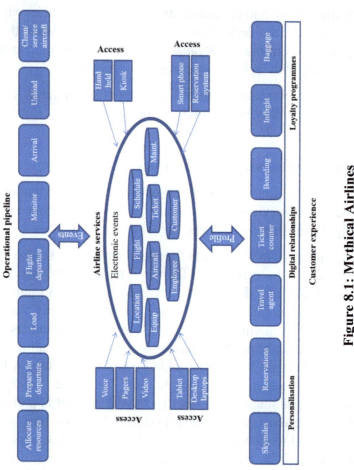

Figure 8.1: Mythical Airlines

Now, which of the services we mention is a business service and which is IT? The answer is that all are business services that depend on IT and the 'IT services' and organisational units all must support the lines of business of the air carrier.

Perspectives

Using Mythical Airlines as an example, the users might have requested that customers of the airline, the passengers, are enrolled in a frequent flyer programme that links with other airlines; the board (Governance) might well have approved this service request. The design session (Strategy), however, noted that it would be too expensive to invest in the software and the IT infrastructure needed to partner with other airlines and thus identified that Mythical should launch a service that provided the frequent flyer programme but was predicated on joining up with other partners at a later time.

Remember that Mythical has many automated and non-automated services, as well as many services that might not at first be perceived as airline services, such as employing cooks to work in the executive lounge where the service is providing food for passengers who have status in the Mythical frequent flyer programme.

Who *really* are the stakeholders? Mythical might be part of an airline alliance and it is possible that new services are needed to enable more streamlined cooperation such as code sharing of flights. Stakeholders in an airline include shareholders as well as the board of directors.

Partners

In the airline business, air space is a commodity. It is not managed by the airlines but by enterprises that are or were government bodies. The air traffic control bodies cooperate over international air space, or they can be in commercial competition, so airlines using air space will need to have contracts with multiple suppliers of air space. Your business service designer, with the assistance of the SRO, will need to understand Mythical's expansion aspirations and ensure that everyone involved in contractual negotiations understands the impact of sharing numerous IT systems relating to traffic. Air might be free, but the IT systems needed to monitor and predict weather patterns, airport capacity and flight plans certainly are not.

Questions to ask

Are you prepared for change? Whoever is responsible for designing Strategy will need to ensure that each stakeholder considers the following, because the impact of 'service design for airlines' *will* involve IT.

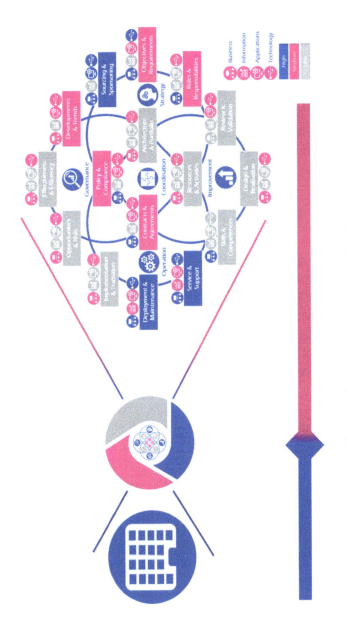

Figure 8.2: Focus, focus, focus (again)

Remember Figure 7.2 from Chapter seven? Well, in this case study, focusing on digital innovation is the main thrust of the exercise.

Think of the four perspectives that we have proposed and apply IT4B as a lens to direct your ideas.

In a class situation, roles will be allotted to participants to assist with clarification about what they should be considering.

Where you are undertaking a strategic business change involving IT, you should know the answers to these questions:

- What is my role?
- What are the objectives of the improvement/innovation/change?
- What are the required new capabilities for the business?
- What are the options?
- What are the benefits?
- What are the costs?
- What are the risks?
- What is required of IT?
- What are the objectives for IT?
- Are there options for the IT change?
- What are the benefits, costs and risks of the IT change?
- Who will direct and manage the programme of change?
- How will the programme be planned and controlled?
- Which parts of the current IT infrastructure should change (organisation, platform, size, responsibility, geography) and which may be retained?
- What should the current IT infrastructure change to?
- How will the changes be managed?

- How do I safeguard long-term IT support to the business?
- What can be done to cope with the change?
- Why should the change be allowed ('what is in this for me?' or for the wider enterprise)?
- Is there any choice?
- Is the investment justified?
- What is the impact on business processing?

This is just the beginning:

- What is the most important change taking place?
- What is the impact on this enterprise?
- What should we be planning for to ensure our long-term future?
- What products and services will be needed?
- What are our current capabilities?
- Can everything be done 'in-house'?
- What new technologies will help us?
- What are our strategic objectives?
- What specific actions must we take and in what timeframe?
- What support will we need?
- What skills are present in the top management team (including the CIO) and what others will we need?
- What kind of action plan can we agree on?
- What will be our communications strategy (internal and external)?
- Can we create a roadmap or model to provide a common picture of the change effort?
- Can we get each senior stakeholder manager to define criteria for success?
- Are there any decisions to be made, or questions to be answered at executive level? What are they?

- Which specific sets of employees will be implementing change and therefore expected to understand the change?
- What new skills will they need?
- Have we communicated the executive, business-level goals effectively?

The SROs in control of the putative enterprise must also direct thinking about planning for change:

- Orchestrate the pace and timing of the strategy.
- Communicate a consistent view.
- Create a central point for information.
- Use sensible, non-generic metrics to monitor progress.
- Make sure that executive action focuses on the links between strategy and operations.
- If necessary, put executives on courses to improve skills in strategic thinking.
- Provide regular updates for middle managers.
- Appoint someone to stay close to the programme managers or leading teams to stay on top of issues and to ensure that no mixed messages are communicated.

Key points

Understand that there is a difference between communicating what is to happen and expecting it to happen.

Make sure the overall vision is simple and inspiring, but not constricting.

Understand whether the change is being driven by external factors (and what they are) and that it is understood at executive level.

Transactions

Essentially, you are collaborating about business service design to ensure that digital transformation is achieved to the satisfaction of the business. The business, IT and the board are examples of stakeholder groups that need to cooperate in order to achieve the goals of the enterprise. In each of the stakeholder groups, what are the transactions that you require to be fulfilled? To assess the likely satisfaction of stakeholders when transforming, it is often necessary to establish high-level requirements that are known as 'transactions'; these transactions are best described as transactional statements and they need to be considered by each stakeholder group so that the statement is understood, the resource implications are clear and so the transaction can be fulfilled.

Where a transaction cannot be fulfilled (maybe the technology needed to fulfil a requirement is way too expensive), this must be recorded, just as a transaction that can be met is recorded. A comprehensive list of all transactions (successful or not) is essential to maintain cooperation and focus on success.

A transaction may be a request for an element of a service or for a product; fulfilment of that request might require multiple transactions in return.

A single transaction type from a user, for example, Print Passport, might be fulfilled by a supplier response, Print Facilities. The user transaction might, however, be construed as incomplete; in the case of a document that must be secure, the transaction would be better described as Print Secure Passport, requiring the supplier to respond with Secure Print Facilities.

Information service transition will require IT4B to ensure that the services have been fully tested, that users have available to them all necessary documentation that will be needed when the service is in use and that training has been properly carried out. Furthermore, IT4B should ensure that support will be available from trained personnel in the event of problems arising, and that any service desk *(Service & Support)* is fully up to speed with appropriate guidance. Depending on your enterprise policies, you may have separate implementation and transition plans. It is important that these activities are managed, that someone is responsible for signing off that implementation, and transition into use has been successful and accords with plans. Planning might require acquisition of additional resources.

The brilliant **Fred Brooks** stated in his book 'The Mythical Man-Month'; *"Adding manpower to a late software project makes it later."*

Fred Brooks made this even pithier by changing it to *"The bearing of a child takes nine months, no matter how many women are assigned."*

Training and documentation

Training and documentation should be available for users of new services. IT suppliers will be responsible for technical training, though the responsibility for creation and distribution of educational materials and communications should be part of IT4B *(Skills & Competences)*. IT4B should have been involved in every stage of information service design from the initial stakeholder involvement, through creation of the 'design of the design', the exploration of methods such as TOGAF and Agile or other traditional development methods, and, of course, throughout the various testing processes.

It is therefore logical that IT4B should be responsible for ensuring that training is timely and available to those needing to be trained, documentation and user manuals are available (perhaps on paper as well as online) and support is available for users when the new services are delivered.

Fundamentally, you are establishing direction (i.e. how to walk) before you start trotting off into the middle distance with an armful of problems that you will need to address later.

CHAPTER NINE: THE BOTTOM LINE

In the end, digital transformation is constrained only by your vision of what you want and what you (or your enterprise) is willing to pay for. After that it is a matter of establishing coherent business service designs and technology options. It is worthwhile considering the basics, just in case reading this book has fired you with enthusiasm that might be unsustainable in terms of what you can achieve. Let's recap, starting with the definitions.

Transformation

Writing in the Guardian newspaper, Howard King described digital transformation as a wholescale change to the foundational components of a business, from its operating model to its infrastructure. What it sells, to whom and how it goes to market. A transformation programme touches every function of a business; fundamentals from purchasing, finance and human resource, through to operations and technology, sales and marketing.

Managers often forget these fundamentals because the responsibility for digital business moves rapidly around in the enterprise as new ideas are thrown in or problems arise. Responsibilities that once belonged to the chief information officer are increasingly the chief marketing officer's. These executives can be new to the world of digital business, having little experience managing in a digital environment. Some would say that isn't necessarily a bad thing, because whereas some with years of experience may take the fundamentals for granted, many of the new executives leading digital initiatives may not.

What fundamentals are digital leaders most at risk of missing? There are three particular business basics that managers can forget, but the first, the *absolute* first thing to remember, is that when beginning a digital business initiative, be sure you know *why* you are beginning it and what the business goals are. A business case is vital, but the initial collaboration on the outcomes of the business service redesigns must be established.

1. Do not forget the business case. Do not become so focused on the technological aspects of digital business that technology purchase takes priority over the necessity to improve the way the company does business. Digital transformation is only partially about technology; it is, as we have mentioned throughout, about using new technology to enable novel or more effective business strategies. Many people believe that they need to be in emerging technologies without being able to clearly articulate why they need to invest in these technologies – or what business purpose they could serve.

2. Executive support is key for success. Managers who aren't directly involved in technology functions often assume that they are not digital managers. However, as the enterprise begins to engage in digital business, all managers must become digital managers. Whether directly involved in implementing the technology or not, managers must understand the business case for digital initiatives and what other aspects of the enterprise need to be aligned to accomplish those goals. As mentioned in this book and in others we have written, when executives simply delegate responsibility for IT/digital business to the technologists, it is a recipe for near-certain failure. Executive involvement in and direct

support for digital business initiatives signal to the enterprise that these initiatives are important; setting goals can therefore begin in earnest. Training will be essential. Consider who needs most training: executives who don't believe they have the technological knowledge to effectively lead or support digital initiatives, or technologists lacking the managerial experience and strategic insight they would need to lead digital business efforts effectively.

3. Strong executive support does not guarantee successful delivery. A mandate from the top is not a magic spell. As many writers have pointed out, if you simply expect employees to engage in new digital business processes because your company adopts a new digital platform, you are hallucinating. They won't. Employees typically do not have either the time or the knowledge to identify new ways to work in the context of their existing job responsibilities.

Employees should be provided with adequate training to learn to engage the technology and digital processes effectively. Consider new ways of learning (online, for example); consider also moving people around to learn from others.

People must be given time and space to adapt. Employees are very good at sticking with established ways of doing things because they are safe and familiar. New ways of working require thinking and people very often want to be told what to do or rely on experience. Change is never good, but everyone likes to improve.

Incidentally we all know that businesses often build and develop new products and services, move into new markets, acquire, merge with or sell to competitors, or change the components from their value chain to gain competitive advantage, but none of these things are digitally transformative. Or any other version of transformative really; these are common and accepted ways of improving revenue. Evolving with and over time. Digital transformation requires planning and involves greater risk and often a lot of money, and often becomes a necessity.

Why? Because most enterprises must experience a traumatic transformation when they have failed to evolve. When a business evolves with its market, continually refreshing products and services and reaching new sets of customers, it doesn't need to transform.

The key drivers of transformation

There are three key drivers of transformation: changing consumer demand, changing technology and changing competition. These, of course, are part of an ever-evolving ecosystem and it is always a melting pot of factors that cause changes in a market.

When any of these factors coincide, such that the operating model of the enterprise is no longer fit to serve its customers, the business has reached a tipping point. And as we mention above, evolving businesses don't reach tipping points. Evolving businesses are continually focused on their customers, changing and adapting with, or leading their market. Businesses that spot tipping points when they are too late to be considered opportunities need to transform, and those that don't, tip over the edge.

Clearly, none of this is new. So it is a bit of a surprise that many enterprises fail to notice doom creeping up on them.

Define digital

In the widest sense 'digital' can be defined as any technology that connects people and machines with one another or with information. Therefore 'digital transformation' is a dramatic and public restructure to avoid a tipping point caused by digital technologies and market effects ignored by otherwise smart executives.

Most of the large global consultancies manage transformation programmes on behalf of large businesses. To transform a large enterprise takes a significant amount of time, a huge amount of resources and a cross-functional set of business skills that are found in global consultancies.

Smaller consultancies work with their clients to see what's coming and help them evolve to meet the future. They help to bring new ideas, products and services to life in prototypes so that businesses can imagine the future, be ready for the future and perhaps, in some cases, be ready to lead the markets.

APPENDIX A: THEORIES ABOUT ORGANISATIONAL CHANGE

Let's look at some theories about organisational change, starting with the 'traditional' picture where Strategy (A1) sits at the apex and then explain how we think IT4B can help.

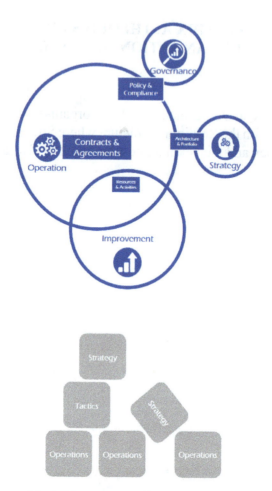

Figure A1: Ad hoc enterprise – bottom-up strategy

At first, there is the reality that most enterprises are a little chaotic and though they may aim to be more organised, they often make a mess in the pursuit of digital effectiveness. Strategy is often generated bottom-up. If the ultimate goal is becoming a digital enterprise, getting there requires rather more organisation.

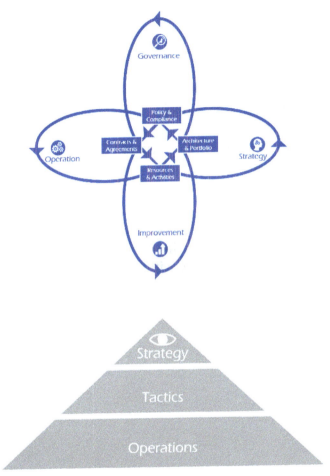

Figure A2: Analytic enterprise – top-down strategy

Figure A2 is most likely familiar to anyone who has read any book on management or IT management. This represents what is often described as the analytic enterprise, exemplified to a large extent by the principles of scientific management, a.k.a. Taylorism – as described by Frederick Winslow Taylor in the early 20th century.

Typical characteristics of analytical enterprises include a 'Theory-X posture' towards staff, which is a mechanistic view of organisational structure, functional silos, local optimisation and a management focus on, for example, costs and 'efficiencies'. Middle-managers are seen as owners of the way the business works, channelling executive intent, allocating work and reporting on progress, within a command-and-control style regime. The analytic mindset recognises that the way work is done has some bearing on costs and the quality of the results.

Designing strategy is considered a highly complex process that has to be carried out top-down and can take several months or even years to implement. Transformation to a digital enterprise therefore will most likely be regarded as a time-consuming, idealistic process that can never really be achieved.

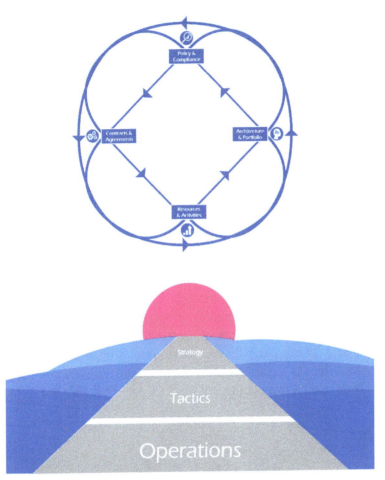

Figure A3: Synergistic enterprise – roadmap strategy

Figure A3 is where we can see the strategy, tactics and operations labels disappearing into the sunset; imagine these things more as a road that is travelled.

Sometimes also referred-to as 'holistic', synergistic enterprises exemplify, to some extent, the principles of the Lean movement. Typical characteristics include a 'Theory-

Y orientation' (characterised at least in their internal propaganda as respect for people), an organic, emergent, complex-adaptive-system view of organisational structure, and an enterprise-wide focus on learning, flow of value and effectiveness.

Middle-managers are respected for their experience and domain knowledge, coaching the workforce in, for example, building self-organising teams, and systemic improvement efforts. The synergistic mindset realises that individual tasks within an enterprise are co-dependent on one another, and only have relevance in getting some larger end-to-end purpose accomplished.

Strategy is often referred to as a 'roadmap', designed through co-creation where leadership leads by example. A roadmap can be stretched out over several years and is often translated into different departmental roadmaps, such as an IT roadmap, which makes managing consistency between versions quite a challenge. This complexity often calls for heavy-duty enterprise architecture and portfolio capabilities, which can have a negative impact on enterprise agility.

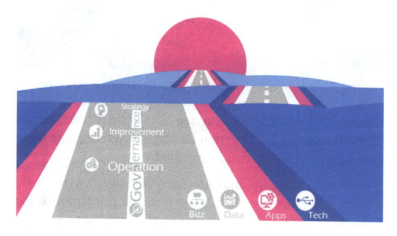

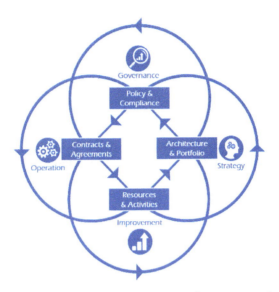

Figure A4: Chaordic (digital) enterprise – strategic focus

The chaordic mindset (Figure A4) believes that being too organised, structured, ordered and regimented often means being too slow to respond effectively to new opportunities and threats. A chaordic enterprise will attempt to operate balanced at the knife-edge of maximum effectiveness, on the optimal cusp between orderly working and chaotic collapse.

This requires a strategy design that is a very Agile, short-cyclic process, which can adapt quickly to new challenges and developments (following the contours of the landscape so to speak), but with a clear strategic focus.

Why IT4B?

We believe the IT4B model is of value in any enterprise. Within a chaordic enterprise this value is particularly easy to demonstrate. The IT4B operating model can function as a virtual gyroscope, spinning over several axes, keeping the enterprise focused on the horizon. Though Strategy leads upfront and has a focus a little bit closer to the horizon, Improvement follows closely with Operation not far behind. Governance monitors if everything is still on track. The shorter the cycle and the more often it is completed, the more balanced and Agile the organisation will be.

This is the way we look at the big picture of IT4B: balancing resources, maintaining equilibrium and identifying what is needed to transform business using that horrible IT stuff.

APPENDIX B: USEFUL POINTERS IN FORMULATING BUSINESS AND IT STRATEGY

General

How might our IT strategy constrain sourcing options?

What is our future technical direction or strategy?

What technology issues need to be considered?

Are we constrained by legacy systems?

How important is the service?

What impact does it have on the business?

Is it core or non-core, strategic or useful?

Can we regard the service as a commodity? Or does it differentiate us in some way?

Requirement focus

Is the requirement oriented towards acquiring resources that we will manage?

Or is it oriented towards a defined result, outcome or defined level of service performance?

What benefits are sought: is the emphasis on cost savings or on improvement in business value?

Demand focus

How sure are we of future requirements?

With what degree of confidence can we predict demand and service volumes?

How do we envisage the services and our requirements might develop?

Are they stable or is there scope for innovation?

Purchasing approach

Are we seeking to establish an ongoing relationship?

Or do we see future requirements more as a series of transactions, each of which will be completed?

Service definition

How tightly can we specify requirements for the information services?

Is only a loose definition possible or appropriate?

Will we be able to measure performance? How?

Current service performance

How does current service performance (which may be in-house or contracted out) compare with the market as a whole?

What scope is there for improvement?

Are there any opportunities to exploit economies of scale?

Can this be achieved internally?

What is the current state of the market?

Degrees of integration

How closely integrated is the service with others?

How integral to our business processes is it?

Could we separate it out?

If something goes wrong, would the impact be isolated from other business activities?

Technology familiarity and maturity

How mature is the service and the technology that underpins it?

How familiar are we with the technology?

Business partners and vendors are also key stakeholders in managing the programme/project portfolio. Most of the time, enterprises involve their business partners and/or vendors in executing various programmes/projects. Hence it is very important to involve them, to the extent needed, in the communications.

APPENDIX C: A COMMUNICATIONS STRATEGY

A communications strategy, irrespective of target audience, has broadly the same motivation: it defines how communications will be established and managed during the running of the policy delivery. Developing the Strategy will involve:

- Confirming the identity of the relevant stakeholders and their needs;
- Identifying the information to be communicated, both outwards from the programme and inwards to the programme from the stakeholders;
- Selecting the appropriate way(s) of communicating to each (for example, briefings, newsletters, presentations), and the required frequencies; and
- Defining the associated costs and including these in the overall budget.

Communication is central to any change (or improvement) process – the greater the amount of change, the greater the need for clear communication about the reasons, benefits, plans and proposed effects of that change. It is important, therefore, that the communications strategy should be defined and implemented as early as possible and then adequately maintained throughout the programme.

The communications for your overall business strategy should answer the following questions:

- What are the objectives of the communications?
- What are the key messages?
- Who are you trying to reach?
- What information will be communicated?

- When will information be disseminated, and what are the relevant timings?
- How much information will be provided, and to what level of detail?
- What mechanisms will be used to disseminate information?
- How will feedback be encouraged, and what will be done as a result of feedback?
- What central initiatives or policies must we respond to?
- How have these constrained or enabled sourcing options?
- Are there any planned legislative or policy changes that could affect the services we require?
- What is the future of our core business?
- What are our corporate aims and objectives?
- Can we identify some activities as non-core?

In addition, a subsection focused on digital aspirations should drill down into technical (applications/services and technology) issues relating to the IT part of the strategy.

APPENDIX D: SKILLS

Successful delivery skills framework

A skills framework is one of the major products of a successful delivery skills (SDS) programme. It includes definition of a matrix that identifies the target benchmark level of maturity for each skill area across a range of project roles.

Possible maturity levels

The SDS programme should recognise at least three levels of maturity in each of the individual skills. These could be similar to a Foundation – level 1, a Practitioner – level 2 and perhaps an Expert – level 3 maturity, though criteria must be carefully thought through. An expert is not someone who can memorise a few books and pass exams based on multiple choice answers.

How the framework could be designed

The framework could catalogue all the necessary skills in a small(ish) number of categories:

- Generic skills
- The business environment
- Contractual relationships
- Programme and project delivery
- Technical skills
- The legal environment

For each of the skills areas, the framework provides a description of the main (minimum) subject areas that have been identified as residing under the specific skill. In most cases, these areas would be the same for both Level 1 and 2, the difference being the depth to which the participant is expected to know each subject matter. Where the subject matter expands from Level 1 to Level 2, this must be listed in the framework.

There is then a short description of the training required to develop the participant's capability, using the target – what the module is to teach – and the 'learning outcomes' – what the participant will be able to do differently as a result of the training.

How to use the framework

The framework is initially used to provide a description of each skill level when assessing a participant against a maturity matrix to find a starting level for each skill area. It can also be used to identify skills areas an individual may need to address, should they wish to tackle a particular career path. You most likely need:

- Skills framework
- Skill area
- Specific skill
- Generic skills

Generic skills are relatively easy to identify and some ideas are provided below.

Leadership

Teamwork
Interpersonal skills
Risk management
Communication
The business environment

Finance

The business case
Commercial business and finance
Disposal of assets
Selling of services
Commercial negotiation
Contractual relationships

Programme and project delivery

Programme management and project management have substantial overlaps in terms of the subjects to be addressed. One of the key differences is the context within which the subjects are presented. There are also substantial interdependencies at a programme level.

- Programme management
- Project management
- Managing business change
- Benefits management

Technical and other skills; take a look at the skills/competence you might expect to see in a CIO, someone who frequently will be the SRO of a programme of innovative change.

Specific responsibilities

The CIO/SRO should perform the following key, high-level functions:

- Ensuring that programmes/projects are subject to review at appropriate stages;

- Making certain that any recommendations or concerns from reviews are met or addressed before progressing to the next stage;
- Developing the project or programme brief and business case;
- Overseeing the development of the brief for the change and business case;
- Ensuring that the aims of the planned change continue to be aligned with the business, and establishing a firm basis for the project or programme during its initiation and definition;
- Securing the necessary investment for the business change;
- Developing the project or programme enterprise structure and logical plans; and
- Engaging with the work of either project initiation (in a project environment), or establishing the programme (in a programme environment).

An SRO must be someone who can:

- Broker relationships with stakeholders within and outside the project;
- Deploy delegated authority to ensure that the project achieves its objectives;
- Provide advice and guidance to the project manager(s) as necessary;
- Acknowledge their own skill/knowledge gaps and structure the project board and project management team accordingly;
- Provide the time required to perform the role effectively; and
- Negotiate well and influence people.

We could add 'walk on water and change water into wine', but you get the idea. *Skills & Competences* pervades the entirety of the enterprise. A hole in the framework can seriously jeopardise outcomes demanded by Governance authorities and expected by Operations.

APPENDIX E: THOUGHTS ABOUT TESTING THE DESIGN OF SERVICES

Test management

Purpose

It is the role of test management to ensure that new or modified digital services or products or even new hardware meets the business requirements for which they have been developed or enhanced.

The purpose of test management is to ensure that a testing strategy is both devised and applied that is efficient, effective and economic.

The testing strategy should define the objectives of all test stages and the techniques that apply. The testing strategy also forms the basis for the creation of a standardised documentation set, and facilitates communication of the test process and its implications outside of the test discipline. Any test support tools introduced should be aligned with, and support, the test strategy.

Test management is also concerned with both test resource and test environment management.

Key elements of test management

These include:

- Test enterprise – the setup and management of a suitable test organisational structure and explicit role definition. The project framework under which the testing activities will be carried out is reviewed, high-level test phase plans prepared and resource schedules considered. Test enterprise also involves the determination of configuration standards and the definition of the test environment.

- Test planning – the requirements definition and design specifications facilitate in the identification of major test items and these may necessitate updating the test strategy. A detailed test plan and schedule is prepared with key test responsibilities being indicated.
- Test specifications – required for all levels of testing and covering all categories of test. The required outcome of each test must be known before the test is attempted.
- Unit, integration and system testing – configuration items are verified against the appropriate specifications and in accordance with the test plan. The test environment should also be under configuration control and test data and results stored for future evaluation.
- Test monitoring and assessment – ongoing monitoring and assessment of the integrity of the development and construction. The status of the configuration items should be reviewed against the phase plans and test progress reports prepared providing some assurance of the verification and validation activities.
- Product assurance – the decision to negotiate the acceptance testing programme and the release and commissioning of the service product is subject to the 'product assurance' role being satisfied with the outcome of the verification activities. Product assurance may oversee some of the test activity and may participate in process reviews.

Fitness for purpose checklist

Is there a documented test strategy that defines the objectives of all test stages and the techniques that may apply, e.g. non-functional testing and the associated techniques such as performance, stress and security, etc.?

Does the test plan prescribe the approach to be taken for intended test activities, identifying:

- The items to be tested;
- The testing to be performed;
- Test schedules;
- Resource and facility requirements;
- Reporting requirements;
- Evaluation criteria; and
- Risks requiring contingency measures.

Are test processes and practices reviewed regularly to assure that the testing processes continue to meet specific business needs? For example, innovative e-commerce testing may involve new user interfaces, and a business focus on usability may mean that the enterprise must review its testing strategies.

Testing and commissioning is often inadequately considered by project teams and is pressurised by available time and resources, particularly towards project completion.

It is essential that sufficient time and suitable resources are dedicated to testing and commissioning to assure the project's fundamental success. There are advantages in using dedicated, specialist resources, i.e. independent of the development/construction team, and the project sponsor should ensure that testing requirements are considered throughout the project lifecycle and a suitable test strategy and appropriate test plans are formulated and instantiated.

Source information

Business requirements including success criteria.

Project plans including detailed phase/stage plans and schedules.

Requirements definition.

Design specification.

Operability standards.

Implementation strategy and release plans.

Customer acceptance criteria.

Customer acceptance test specification.

APPENDIX F: PERFORMANCE

You will definitely and unequivocally need performance measures to cover all aspects of a service arrangement:

- Costs, benefits realised and value obtained.
- Performance and customer satisfaction.
- Delivery improvement and quantified added value.
- Delivery capability.
- Success criteria.
- Relationship strength and responsiveness.

It is important that the measures of performance you choose (and that really should be specified in the contract and in any SLA) offer clear and demonstrable evidence of the success (or otherwise) of the relationship.

Once chosen, the requirements, or questions, that lead to knowing that underpinning performance measures have been met, should be the primary focus for contract management. They should provide the framework around which provider information requirements and flows, contract management teams, skills, processes and activities are developed.

It is necessary to have an existing baseline against which to track any performance measures that are related to delivery or capability improvement. Much of this baseline will typically be established in the business case for whatever service has been procured or is being designed.

Three levels of performance assessment are often used:

- The base level concerned with ongoing service delivery using conventional SLA approaches and related measures.

- The middle level comprising the desired results of individual programmes of change or improvement, implementation of projects or developments and infrastructure rollouts carried out during the period of the deal. Measures at this level are likely to be derived from investment appraisal and benefits management techniques and constructed on a case-by-case basis.
- At the highest level an enterprise is concerned with the overall outcome or impact of the deal: what do we want to have achieved by the end of the contract period? These measures will be derived from the objectives identified during project scoping and in the preliminary business analysis activity. They will be rooted in your enterprise's long-term business strategy.

Below, we expand on the different levels discussed above to suggest typical performance attributes associated with each level and to categorise types of measure at each level. It is often difficult to distinguish between outcomes and output in practice. An outcome can be the achievement of an improved underlying service delivery capability, whereas an output is fully exploiting that capability in terms of transforming direct service to customers or stakeholders.

Design or procurement details

Strategic objectives.

Organisational change.

Resource use.

Service improvements.

Business performance.

Impact on customers.

Benefits.

Delivery capability.

Process change/improvement.

Effectiveness

Value for money; productivity.

Inputs/outputs.

Acquisition.

Cost.

Delivery timetable.

Outcomes.

Service.

Turnaround.

Availability.

Capacity.

Accuracy.

Quality.

Performance

The range of contracts and agreements you are likely to need include:

- Hardware maintenance services agreement
- System supply agreement
- System supply [framework/enabling] agreement
- System support services agreement
- Product supply terms of agreement

Appendix F: Performance

- Product support services terms
- Information systems/services [framework/enabling] agreement
- Information systems/services agreement
- Software supply agreement
- Software support services agreements

And this list is not definitive.

APPENDIX G: MAINTENANCE

The software maintenance process recognises four classes of software change that will result in upgrades. These are:

- Corrective maintenance – correcting an error found during live running;
- Perfective maintenance – where there are additions, modifications or deletions to the functions of the software to correspond with changes in the business requirement;
- Adaptive maintenance – to allow for changes to the environment such as new systems software or new hardware, but where the functions of the IT service are not changed; and
- Preventive maintenance – carried out to make the software easier to maintain (or to test) in the future.

All changes that result from maintenance must pass through their own development cycle of designing, coding and testing. The requirements for testing changes are, if anything, more stringent than those for new systems. Not only must errors be found in the operation of the features affected by the change but also questions such as 'Has anything been left out?' and 'What other parts of the system are affected?' must be answered.

The preventive maintenance activities in respect of managing the applications and the services they provide include:

Daily:

- Check the use level

- Review daily problem reports
- Review emergency change requests
- Run database consistency checks
- Check database server error logs
- Monitor network performance and errors
- Monitor client status
- Monitor server components and service status
- Monitor event logs of key servers
- Monitor system performance
- Monitor system directories
- Make secure backups of the servers

Weekly:

- Attend appropriate meetings
- Improve database performance
- Check system directories
- Management reports
- File system management

Monthly:

- Write the monthly status report
- Hold work reviews with individual team members
- Review the system status and performance
- Improve system performance
- Secure system accounts
- Review access to server functions
- Undertake recovery tests

Ad hoc:

- Brainstorm improvements with the team
- Complete feedback survey

- Resolve reported problems
- Initiate process improvement actions
- Review reported security infringements
- Improve access control

Optimise

The functional, non-functional and usability requirements of all applications that have been in production should be reviewed periodically. Such a review may be initiated by a trigger:

- Scheduled review in relation to an application portfolio review or an SLA review.
- Issues detected by problem management.
- Changes to the business requirements.
- Changes to the infrastructure.

The review distinguishes a number of areas, such as people, business processes and technology.

AREA/ISSUES

People

Does the application still meet users' needs?

If not, what should be improved?

Is the application intuitive?

Do users make unnecessary mistakes when using the application?

Business process

Has the objective of the supported business process changed? If so, does the application still support it?

Will a change to the organisational structure change the application's functional requirements?

Has there been any change in the service levels?

Technology

Are there any technical problems that result in the application failing to meet the agreed SLAs?

Have any infrastructure changes been made that require changes to the application?

What is the application performance? Is any improvement required?

What are the availability and manageability of the application like?

To what extent does the application support the service support processes?

The use of an application portfolio can make it much easier to deal with these questions. The following decisions can be taken further to the review:

- No change required
- The application will be changed
- The application will be phased out

FURTHER READING

IT Governance Publishing (ITGP) is the world's leading publisher for governance and compliance. Our industry-leading pocket guides, books, training resources and toolkits are written by real-world practitioners and thought leaders. They are used globally by audiences of all levels, from students to C-suite executives.

Our high-quality publications cover all IT governance, risk and compliance frameworks and are available in a range of formats. This ensures our customers can access the information they need in the way they need it.

Other publications that may be of interest include

- Collaborative Business Design
  www.itgovernancepublishing.co.uk/product/collaborati
  ve-business-design
- Running IT Like a Business
  www.itgovernancepublishing.co.uk/product/running-it-
  like-a-business
- Pragmatic Application of Service Management
  www.itgovernancepublishing.co.uk/product/pragmatic-
  application-of-service-management

For more information on ITGP and branded publishing services, and to view our full list of publications, please visit www.itgovernancepublishing.co.uk.

To receive regular updates from ITGP, including information on new publications in your area(s) of interest, sign up for our newsletter at
www.itgovernancepublishing.co.uk/topic/newsletter.

Branded publishing

Through our branded publishing service, you can customise ITGP publications with your company's branding.

Find out more at

www.itgovernancepublishing.co.uk/topic/branded-publishing-services.

Related services

ITGP is part of GRC International Group, which offers a comprehensive range of complementary products and services to help organisations meet their objectives.

For a full range of resources related to the topics covered in this book visit www.itgovernance.co.uk/information.

Training services

The IT Governance training programme is built on our extensive practical experience designing and implementing management systems based on ISO standards, best practice and regulations.

Our courses help attendees develop practical skills and comply with contractual and regulatory requirements. They also support career development via recognised qualifications.

Learn more about our training courses and view the full course catalogue at www.itgovernance.co.uk/training .

Professional services and consultancy

We are a leading global consultancy of IT governance, risk management and compliance solutions. We advise businesses around the world on their most critical issues and present cost-saving and risk-reducing solutions based on international best practice and frameworks.

We offer a wide range of delivery methods to suit all budgets, timescales and preferred project approaches.

Find out how our consultancy services can help your organisation at www.itgovernance.co.uk/consulting.

Industry news

Want to stay up to date with the latest developments and resources in the IT governance and compliance market? Subscribe to our Daily Sentinel newsletter and we will send you mobile-friendly emails with fresh news and features about your preferred areas of interest, as well as unmissable offers and free resources to help you successfully start your projects. www.itgovernance.co.uk/daily-sentinel.

EU for product safety is Stephen Evans, The Mill Enterprise Hub, Stagreenan, Drogheda, Co. Louth, A92 CD3D, Ireland. (servicecentre@itgovernance.eu)

www.ingramcontent.com/pod-product-compliance
Lightning Source LLC
Chambersburg PA
CBHW071109050326
40690CB00008B/1163